Beginner's Guide
to Archery

Beginner's Guide
to Archery

TOM FOY

PELHAM BOOKS

First published in Great Britain by
PELHAM BOOKS LTD
52 Bedford Square
London, W.C.1
1972

© *1972 Tom Foy*

7207 0454 5

*Printed in Great Britain by
Northumberland Press Ltd., Gateshead,
and bound by Dorstel Press, Harlow*

This book is dedicated to my wife,
Rose, who is long-suffering in the
cause of my archery

Contents

Illustrations

Introduction

Why on earth should anyone want to take up archery in this day and age? The bow is far inferior to the rifle in speed and accuracy, and if you had to catch your dinner with it you would probably starve before you had got the knack. In a world of laser beams, supersonic airliners, and space satellites, it does at first sight seem a bit strange that people should take up a hobby which involves propelling little bits of wood through the air with the aid of a string on a bigger piece of wood, but that is what it amounts to. Perhaps it is the very fact that it is old-fashioned and belongs to a world gone by that first attracts people. Although they might not readily admit it, lots of them take up the sport because of the romantic past it has had, Robin Hood, Sherwood Forest, and all that. Perhaps another part of the answer is that people want to take up a sport which gets back to something basic where an individual is dependent entirely on his own inner resources. Archery is certainly a sport for the individual. Whether you have a good or bad day, it does not affect your companions' shooting by a single point.

Whatever the reasons for it, the fact remains that people *are* taking up archery, and in larger numbers than they ever have before. And when they get into the sport, they find that it is no longer 'olde worlde', but that it is a very modern sport indeed. It is now included in the Olympic Games, there are regular World Championships, and it is quite often to be seen on television, so I am sure that it will continue to grow into a popular and modern sport.

One of the most important points contributing to the growth of archery in recent years is that it can be enjoyed by such a wide range of ages. One hears every day of the troubles caused by the 'generation gap', but in my own club we have several members of sixteen and others over sixty and they get on perfectly well together. Perhaps we might have arguments if we were to discuss politics or religion, but we don't; we talk about archery. Because archery can be taken up at almost any age it means that all the members of a family can shoot together. In how many other sports can Mum and Dad and all their growing children take part, and on equal terms? Lots of people think that because they have reached middle age they can no longer think about taking up a new sport, but as far as archery is concerned this is not so. At one British Championship meeting at Oxford an old lady of ninety was shooting, and when another archer offered to retrieve her arrows for her, she replied that when she was too old to pick her arrows up from the ground she would stop shooting them. So if you are still a youngster in your sixties you could still have years of pleasant shooting ahead of you.

I have been an archer now for nearly twenty years. Naturally I started off as a poor shot, everyone does; in fact it took me two and a half years to reach the lowest standard, Third Class. These days this standard is normally achieved in the first season. Eventually I became a Master Bowman, held it for six years, and now I am back to being mediocre again, but the sport hasn't lost any of its appeal for me. If work prevents me from shooting for a month or two I feel a certain restlessness, so that I have to get my bow out to give it a polish, and check the arrows to see if any of the fletchings need replacing. If I'm on holiday and I spot a field with some targets in I can't help going over to have a look to see what the club is like. You see, the sport gets a hold on you like a drug, and you can't give it up, nor do you wish to.

In this book I have tried to convey to the reader how this sport appeals so much. As you read each chapter, not only will you be finding out about the sport, but I hope you get the feeling that being an archer is something special; I certainly do. There are two things about the sport that I have deliberately left out; the first is the history of archery, and the second is the making of equipment. The reason for this is that both these subjects would need a great deal of space to deal with them adequately, and there are already several excellent books available which were written by experts in these subjects and anything written by myself would make a poor comparison. What I have tried to do is to describe the modern sport as it is known to the average club archer, in the hope that it will draw more people from all walks of life into the hobby which has given me so many years of fun and good companionship.

1. *How to get started*

When you first take the decision that you are going to take up the sport of archery you may feel that it is something that you could do quite satisfactorily in your own back garden, but you would be wrong; you will soon tire of the sport if you do not join a club.

Even if you are fortunate enough to have a garden large enough for you to shoot in you will soon lose interest without other people to share the fun of shooting, and with whom you can compare your scores. Until you join a club you will be cut off from better archers than yourself who could give you hints and tips that could improve your scores, and the mere fact of shooting with people who are able to beat you will give you an incentive to improve.

It is very easy to find out where your nearest club is. Simply write to the secretary of the Grand National Archery Society whose address is on page 146 at the back of the book and he will let you know. If your nearest club is too far away for you to reach there is a chapter later on that tells you how to start your own club from scratch, so there is no excuse for shooting in solitary confinement in your own garden.

Whichever club you finally decide on, it is important that you go to one that has somebody able to coach you in your early attempts, for it is much easier to teach a beginner the right way to shoot than to correct faults later on that he has adopted himself in his early days. Some clubs run an introductory course for newcomers at the beginning of the year so unfortunately people who join later on do not get as much instruction as they would like. Other clubs may have one member who is a coach and is willing to help new archers at any time, but do remember that the archer who takes you under his wing and gives you instruction at your new club is giving up his own shooting in order to help you. It is very annoying to give up one's own chance of shooting in order to help a beginner and then find that he is half an hour late or doesn't turn up at all. It is not much help when he phones later on to say he couldn't make it. So do remember that your instructor is giving you two valuable things; his knowledge, and his own shooting time.

An excellent way of getting started in archery even before you go to a club is to attend a course arranged by the Central Council for Physical Recreation. These courses normally run for two hours on one day a week for six weeks, either in the early evening when there is still plenty of light, or at weekends. The fee for the course is very modest, and they are good value for money, for not only do the participants get expert tuition in shooting, but they pick up a fair amount of other archery knowledge at the same time. During breaks in the shooting there will be lessons in bowstring making, fletching, which is the technical term for attaching feathers to arrow shafts, the rules of shooting, and other kindred subjects; so that when a newcomer finishes the course he can go to any club safe in the knowledge that he will not feel quite such a new boy as perhaps he might have done.

An increasing number of Evening Institutes are now including archery amongst their lists of subjects taught, but as an evening class lasts for a whole year the acquisition of knowledge is slower than one would find in a C.C.P.R. course. Many of the class members are quite content with their one evening a week and have little wish to go further with the sport. I have taught in various evening classes over many years and I have always found it difficult to persuade evening class members to join a club. My classes usually have as many members at the end of the year as at the beginning, so I am sure that they enjoy their archery, but all the while they are able to rejoin when the new term starts they simply will not go to a club. The idea behind the C.C.P.R. courses seems to be that the coaches have six weeks to turn these people into archers and then they have to join a club. The course ends after the sixth week, and then they must join a club or cease shooting. The moral of all this is that if you start your archery

at an Evening Institute pick up as much knowledge and shooting skill as you can, but as soon as the fair weather time of the
year comes around, then join a club. The shooting you do at
the evening institute will still be of great benefit to you, but it
is a supplement to your club shooting, not a substitute for it.

The final way of obtaining your initial archery knowledge is
to attend a course organized by the coaching branch of the
Grand National Archery Society. Details of the next course
can be obtained by writing to the secretary, but generally
these courses are held during a weekend from Friday night
until Sunday evening, and these are a very concentrated form
of tuition, for besides the shooting, which obviously forms the
basis of any course, there are film shows, lectures, discussions,
and demonstrations; and sometimes the discussions get very
animated and go on late into the evening. Unfortunately,
absolute beginners rarely get to hear of these courses until
they have been shooting for a little while, so the participants
usually come under the heading of 'improvers' rather than
'beginners'.

If you were to ask me which of all these ways of starting
shooting is best I would plumb for going to the club. The
tuition will probably be inferior to the other methods unless
it has a good coach, but you will be learning in the company
of people who are going to be your future shooting friends,
and you will soon begin to feel like an 'old hand' in the club.

2. *Choosing the right equipment*

In every sport where it is one man against the rest it is most important for the equipment to be just the right size for the particular person using it, but I can think of none where it is more critical than in archery. An archer's equipment is as exactly right for him as his clothes are, and just as you would not expect to get Hardy into one of Laurel's suits, so you could not expect an archer to shoot well with another person's equipment. If a coat fits badly, everyone can see it straight away, but in archery a newcomer cannot immediately adopt a perfect style, so it takes a few hours of shooting under instruction before what is right for this particular archer can be decided. It follows that it is so much better to use borrowed equipment right at the beginning even if it is only for one lesson, than to rush out to buy your own equipment and probably get the wrong specification.

When you have been told by your coach, or got a pretty good idea for yourself, what size of equipment you need, it is always sound policy to use a store that either specializes in archery or has at least a special department for it, with someone in charge qualified to give advice. If you use a store which has just a few bows and three or four sets of arrows for the occasional enquiry they will sell you what they have got in stock, not what is right for you. This happened to me when I first started shooting. I purchased a wooden bow, three arrows, and a book from my local small sports store and went off to a nearby wood full of the wildest enthusiasm. Half an hour later, having lost all three arrows, I started reading the book and found that the arrows I had just lost were about six inches too short for me. Even now I can remember buying dowelling, fletchings, etc., and making some more arrows the correct size according to what was said in the book, and then fitting one to the bow and drawing back. Of course the bow couldn't take it and snapped in half, so I was just about back to square one. Why I didn't immediately take up rifle shooting I cannot recall. So learn from my mistakes and go to a specialist.

Although actually shooting under the instruction of a coach is the best way of determining your choice of equipment, it is possible to give some guidelines to somebody who has no choice but to sort it out for himself. If there is no one to help you, then the first thing for you to discover is your correct length of arrow; everything else comes after this.

A fairly accurate method of finding this most important measurement is shown in PLATE 1. Place the end of a dowel against your chest and level with your shoulders. Stretch your arms forward and hold the dowel between your finger tips. The arrow you require is one inch longer than where your fingers have reached. This method is obviously not so good as measuring the arrow length when you are in the correct shooting position shown in PLATES 2 and 3, but it is so difficult for a beginner to get this position exactly right that the finger tip method is best at the start.

If you cannot quite make up your mind which of two lengths is best for you then get the longer one. If you find during your shooting that when you are in the correct position an inch or two of the arrow is sticking forward of the bow, don't worry, it will simply mean that the arrow will not go quite so far, or will lose 'cast' as archers say. It is a mistake to try to draw an arrow to its full length if this means that you lose the correct position, for you can shoot quite accurately with two inches of arrow ahead of the bow provided that your style is correct. There is no danger in shooting with arrows that appear to be too long, but it is most decidedly dangerous to use arrows that are too short, and for this reason: when you draw back you will be looking at the target, and with a short arrow you may possibly draw the point back too far and not notice it come inside the bow. When you loose, the point will stick into the bow, preventing the arrow from going forward, and the pressure from the string will shatter the arrow with possible injury to yourself from the pieces.

Even if you never draw inside the bow, shooting with arrows that are too short will tend to make you shoot in a hunched, cramped style that will be difficult to cure later on.

A word on what is meant by arrow-length would not be out of place here. Archers often complain that the arrows they have been sold are half an inch longer than the measurement stated on the box. This is because manufacturers wisely measure only that part of the arrow which is going to be drawn by the archer. The slot of the nock is about one quarter of an inch deep, and the rounded part of the point is another quarter of an inch, and neither of these will be drawn, so an arrow is always half an inch longer than the amount the archer actually draws. Half an inch is not going to matter much to a beginner, but it can be quite important to a Master Bowman, so do remember that when we talk about arrow-length we really mean draw-length.

When you have found your correct draw-length you can go ahead and purchase your arrows, which are normally sold in sets of eight. This is because they are shot in groups of six, called an 'end', which leaves you with two extra to act as spares in case of damage or loss. The cheapest arrows that can be bought are made of wood, but you will find them a false economy, for they break easily and will warp with time. A wooden arrow which has snapped should never be repaired because it is bound to go again on a later shot, with the possibility of slivers of wood being driven into the archer's hand. The most popular material for arrows at the present time is strong tubular aluminium alloy, and without a doubt these are the better buy. They are available in a wide range of prices according to the amount of care put into their manufacture, but don't waste your money by purchasing an expensive set, instead get the very cheapest you can find. This first set of arrows is going to get a lot of very hard use, with more of them going into the ground than on the target, so save your money for a better set later on when your skill has improved. After several months of shooting, these arrows will probably have become bent from the stones you have hit in the ground, but they can be straightened quite cheaply by the manufacturer and given a new lease of life. It is a mistake to try to straighten them yourself without the aid of a straightness testing machine, for archers who attempt to straighten alloy arrows by eye frequently put kinks in them that even the man-facturers cannot remove.

The names of all the parts of an arrow are shown in Fig. 1. The feathers are also called 'fletchings,' not flights, and notice particularly that the point is called the 'pile'.

FIG. 1.

Now comes the piece of equipment that I guarantee you will remember for the rest of your life: your first bow. This is the one that will give you so much fun just to shoot, no matter where the arrows go. Later and more expensive bows will bring you high scores and possibly a few prizes, but you will be a fortunate archer if they give you the same pride of possession as this first one. The size of your bow will be determined by your arrow-length, which is the reason for sorting out the arrow-length first, but for each arrow-length there will be a large number of bows all needing different amounts of strength to pull them back; this is called the 'weight' of a bow. When an archer says that the weight of his bow is thirty-six pounds, he means that it takes thirty-six pounds pull to get it back to its full extent, which will be his draw-length. People who have never tried archery always imagine that you have to be very strong to take it up, but of course, you simply buy a bow within your own capabilities. Because people vary so much in strength it is difficult to give advice on what bow weight to buy, but, on the average, a man's first bow should be about thirty pounds and a lady's about twenty-four pounds. I know that most men could probably drag back a bow of sixty pounds while a lady might possibly manage to pull thirty-five, but there is a great deal of difference between drawing a bow with all your veins standing out, and holding comfortably at full draw for ten seconds whilst adjusting minor points in your style. Be modest in your choice of weight; just as a shopping bag is always heavier when you reach home than it was when you left the grocers, so a bow which you drew with ease once or twice in the shop will take a lot more to hold steady at the close of a day's shooting involving 150 arrows.

There is a choice of material in bows as well as in arrows, and again the cheapest type is made of wood. They are mostly 'self' bows, which simply means that they are made from one straight length of wood rather than several layers laminated together, although there will probably be a short extra piece of wood glued to the middle of the bow to give a handle. These bows are good value for money for beginners, although they do 'let down' or lose their weight with time. You can tell if a bow is letting down because it will gradually 'follow the string', or take on a permanent curve when it is unstrung instead of returning to the straight. If you are working to a tight budget then the self-wood bow is the best choice, but if you can afford more then the best beginners' bow of all is the type made from solid glass-fibre, not to be confused with composite bows, which are made from layers of glass-fibre and wood glued together. The solid glass-fibre bows are superior to wood in that the material itself is more resilient than wood and also it allows the bow for any given draw-length to be much shorter than the wood equivalent, both of which contribute towards a much better cast; they never follow the string or lose weight, and I have never heard of one breaking when being used at the proper draw-length. So if your finances will allow it, start off with a solid glass-fibre bow.

A few words of warning here against buying a composite bow, for all of them are fairly expensive, and some of them extremely so. It is my opinion that far too many clubs and coaches encourage beginners to buy composites long before they are really ready for them, and the beginners rapidly become discouraged, because although they have virtually the same equipment as the better archers they cannot get anywhere near the same scores. Although archers will always vary in the speed at which they become proficient, almost all beginners should really spend a complete shooting season with their first bow, certainly until they have reached the standard known as Third Class. As you learn to shoot, your initial awkwardness will disappear and gradually a smooth style will build up. Your muscles will become accustomed to the exercise and you will find that you could manage a few more pounds in draw-weight, so without any doubt you will need to change to a different bow. You will know exactly what draw-length and weight is ideal for you after a year's shooting, and you can purchase a good composite bow which will give you many years of good service. If you buy a composite right at the start, you will find after a few months that you have wasted your money by buying something which is really unsuitable for you.

Having bought your arrows and your bow you will probably have very little money left, but don't worry, there are now only two inexpensive items left that you must have to prevent you from hurting yourself. The first of these is the bracer, and its other name of armguard will tell you that it protects the wrist and forearm from any chance blows that the string might give when the bow is shot. Bracers come in a great variety of designs and materials, shapes, and sizes, but a beginner's bracer should cover a good area and be fairly substantial so that the force of any blows doesn't get through. Experts would rarely hit their arm even without a bracer, but they still invariably wear one in order to keep long sleeves out of the way of the string. The choice of bracer is not very important so long as it is stiff and has straps long enough to go round extra clothing in the winter.

It is worth while spending more time on your choice of tab. This is a specially shaped piece of leather which fits over the fingers that pull the string back; you will see two examples in Fig. 2. The first is the standard tab which has been used for a great number of years; the first and third fingers go through the two holes while the second finger lies in the gap between the holes. The string is pulled back by the first three fingers and the arrow is on the string between the first and second fingers, which is the reason for the slit in the tab at this point.

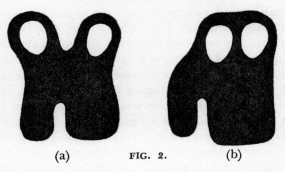

(a)   FIG. 2.   (b)

When the string is released, the rubbing it would normally give to the fingers is transferred instead to the leather of the tab, and so any soreness is avoided. The tab should just be big enough to cover the fingers without overlapping, and at this stage avoid those with an extra thickness sewn on or with leather finger-separators attached. The second example is a recent idea which fits on the second and third fingers, leaving the forefinger free; the reasons for this are explained in the chapter on anchoring. Avoid any form of glove at the present time.

Now we come to four items which are not essential for starting to shoot, but are very useful all the same if you can afford them. Your arrows can be held in a trouser pocket or stuck in the ground beside you, but a cheap quiver with a belt to go round your waist will hold them much more conveniently to hand. A ground-quiver to hold your bow whilst you walk to the target will prevent it from being trodden on accidentally and will keep it away from dirt and damp grass.

Many of your arrows will miss the target and stick in the ground, so a tassle is a handy item for wiping off earth. Before buying one of these from a shop it is worthwhile enquiring to your club secretary about them, for clubs sometimes sell these to members in their own club colours. The quiver, ground-quiver, and tassle can all be made at home if you are any good at handicrafts.

Finally, do get yourself a proper scorebook, and keep a record of your scores right from the beginning. It is very encouraging to see your progress, which is sometimes quick and sometimes slow, and it is reassuring when you hit a bad patch to look up some of your early scores and see just how much better you are now, in spite of the temporary bad patch. I still have my first scores, shot nearly twenty years ago, and they certainly look comic, but I can still remember how much fun I got from shooting those arrows.

3. *Getting your equipment ready*

You now have all the equipment you need to start shooting, and it could be used just as it is, but there are a few jobs on it that can be done at home which will make things much easier when you first visit your club.

A simple thing like stringing your bow can be extremely difficult until you get the knack of it, and it can be embarrassing at your new club if everyone is ready to start shooting and you are still trying to get your bow strung! It doesn't require a great deal of strength if you go about it the right way, so if you follow these instructions carefully you will have no trouble.

First of all, determine which limb of the bow should be at the top, which can be done by looking at the handle. One end of the handle will curve into the bow, while the other end will be flat to support the arrow or may even have a fitted arrow-rest, and this is the top. On many bows one limb will be cut away for the first eight inches or so from the handle; this is called the bow-window and it also denotes the top limb. On self-wood bows the string has a loop around the top limb of the bow and is tied on with a timber hitch at the bottom, but we will assume that you have a solid glass-fibre bow and that the string is supplied separately. This type of string will have a loop at each end. Pass one of these loops over the end of the top limb of the bow and slide it past the two slots cut in the end of the bow, which make up the nock. Pass the other loop over the bottom limb of the bow, but this time fit the loop carefully into the nock, making sure that it is fully in and central. Your string now has its bottom loop in the nock while the top loop is riding free around the upper limb, and you are ready to brace, or string the bow.

Stand with your feet comfortably apart, about twelve to eighteen inches, and place the bottom nock against your left instep, but keep the end of the limb off the ground. Take hold of the bow-handle with your left hand so that the string is away from you; in other words the bow will be between you and the string. Don't grasp the string in addition to the handle; the fingers should be between the string and the bow so that the string is free. Now place the heel of the right hand on the upper limb with the thumb on the left of the limb and the tip of the forefinger on the right side of the limb, both of them just below the loop. Now comes the difficult part. Pull back with your left hand and push forward with the right so that you start to bend the bow. Let the heel of the right hand slide slowly up the limb with the thumb and forefinger pushing the loop ahead of it. As you increase the pressure on the bow you will be able to slide the loop into the nock, but before you relax, make sure that it is seated firmly in both sides of the nock, and take a quick glance down at the bottom nock to make sure the lower loop is still correctly positioned.

The whole of this action is illustrated in PLATE 4, but if you still have difficulty the following points will help you. Most people have no trouble in pushing with the right hand, but forget about pulling equally as hard with the left, so they finish up bent nearly double and still with the loop nowhere near the nock. So don't let the bow get away from you but pull back hard on the handle.

Another common difficulty is caused by pushing the top limb with the web of skin between the thumb and forefinger, which means that the ends of the thumb and forefinger are unable to get near the loop to guide it into the nock. It is the heel of the hand which applies the pressure, with the hand bent back so that the thumb and finger have room to do their job.

Finally, be certain to avoid getting the right hand fingers trapped between the string and the upper limb as you finish nocking, for this will leave you in a very awkward predicament.

Unstringing the bow is almost the same action in reverse, but don't attempt to release the top loop until you have applied enough pressure on the bow to let the string go slack. When this has happened the forefinger will have no trouble in hooking the string from the right side of the nock and then crossing over to do the left, then as you relax, the loop will slide down the limb again.

The first time you brace your bow you will probably find that it takes considerable effort, but when you have managed it five or six times it will come much more easily. Having learned that, we can get on to the next item, which is the fitting of a nocking-point.

If all the arrows are always shot from exactly the same place on the string, they will be much more accurate, so archers mark one particular place; this is the 'nocking-point'. A simple pencil mark could be used to show where to place the arrow, but unfortunately the simple act of drawing back the string is often enough to move the arrow along a little way, so archers bind around the string on either side of the nock to keep the arrow correctly positioned on the same spot.

Brace your bow again, and hold it so that the string is horizontal. In the centre of the string there is a section that has been wound with thread; this is called the 'serving', and its purpose is to protect the main strands of the string from being worn away by the rubbing of the tab and bracer. Place an arrow on the serving so that it hangs down, and the nock should be just tight enough on the string to keep the arrow in place so that a gentle tap on the string is sufficient to dislodge it. If the string is too narrow to hold the nock it will be necessary to put some extra binding underneath the nock as well as either side of it.

Now hold the bow upright and place the arrow on the string again so that the arrow is resting on the top part of the handle, or the fitted arrow-rest if there is one. Move the arrow along the serving until the arrow and the string form a right angle, then move the nock up the string by one eighth of an inch. Mark its position on either side of the nock. Now you have to build up several extra layers of serving either side so that the nock will not be able to slide along during the draw. Ordinary thin cotton will do, although dental-floss, if you can still find any that can be purchased, is far superior because it will lay flat when applied. Start off with a clove hitch and wind the dental-floss quite tightly, and when you have sufficient to keep the arrow in place use another clove hitch to finish off. If the string was able to hold the arrow when you tested it earlier then you will need two separate areas of extra binding, one either side of the nock, but if the arrow fell off then connect them with one or two turns of thread where the nock actually fits. Don't put too much on here, for too thick a nocking-point will be as bad as one too thin, for it will force the sides of the nock apart which will then tend to squeeze itself off the string. See Fig. 3.

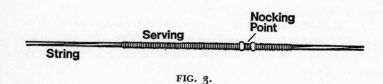

FIG. 3.

If you have used dental-floss instead of cotton you will be able to fuse the cut end by applying a lighted match to it, but do this very carefully to avoid damaging the string, by holding the match over the nocking-point and gently lowering it until the cut end is fused.

There is one last job to be done on the string before moving on, and that is to put a single turn of adhesive tape around the nock of the bottom limb of the bow so that the loop of the string is permanently fixed there. This will prevent the string from coming off and untwisting when the bow is not in use.

Now you can fix a simple sight to the bow. It is possible to find bowsights for sale that cost as much as a composite bow, but at this stage the simplest device will do. A six-inch-long strip of balsa wood will be good enough to hold a pin, and this should be stuck to the top limb of the bow on the surface that will face the target and just above the handle. An even quicker idea is to use a length of surgical tape with a thick piece of string running lengthways underneath it, and this will also be good enough to hold a pin in place. Glass-headed pins are ideal for beginners' bowsights, but failing this an ordinary dress-making pin which has had the head dipped in black paint will suffice.

It is quite likely that there will be no need to do anything at all to your arrows, but you may possibly have to put on them some distinguishing mark. Most arrows are sold with coloured rings painted on them just below the fletchings. These rings are called the 'cresting' and they are there so that each archer can tell his own arrows from all the others. If your arrows are in mass-produced colours or with no cresting at all it would be as well to paint your own rings round them or even put a single band of coloured adhesive tape around each one. It will certainly save any doubt over whose are in the middle and whose are in the grass.

As this whole chapter is concerned with preparation for shooting it would be as well to mention here what clothing to wear for archery. Anything that might interfere with the passage of the bowstring should be avoided, so try to wear something with short sleeves. If cold weather means that you must have long sleeves then make sure that they fit tightly to your arms, and pullovers should fit tightly to the chest. Take a few large elastic bands with you to put around your upper arm if you find that clothing is catching your string, for the slightest touch is all that is needed to ruin a shot.

If you have completed everything in this chapter you are ready to go, so now we can really set about turning you into an archer.

4. *Shooting the first arrow*

There is quite a lot for you to practise before getting to the part where you actually let the arrow go, so most of the instructions for shooting could be practised at home in front of a mirror, stopping short at the loose. Indeed, if you attend any of the beginners' courses described in Chapter 1 you will probably be coached for most of the first lesson before you shoot an arrow at all, so do be patient and get everything right as you go before rushing on to the next part.

A person who is right-handed would normally hold the bow in his left hand and draw the string with his right, but this is not always true, so pick your bow up and see for yourself which feels natural and comfortable. I will assume that you are going to hold the bow in your left, which is most often the case, but if this does not apply to you it should not be difficult to reverse these instructions.

Archers do not stand facing the direction in which they are going to shoot, instead they stand at right angles to it and merely turn their head towards the target. Stand with your feet comfortably apart, in such a position that a line drawn across the front of your toes would extend straight to the centre of the target, as you will see in Fig. 4. Check that you have done this properly, and then keep your feet still. Normally three arrows are shot in succession, and the feet should not be moved from the original position until all three have been loosed. Beginners are particularly prone to shuffling about during shooting and should pay particular attention to this.

Now you have to find the correct position for the hand holding the bow. It should be held quite naturally, almost as though you had picked up a broom which you were handing to someone. There is no need to grip the handle tightly.

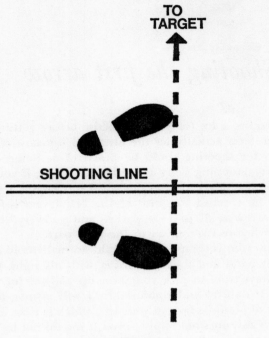

FIG. 4.

Viewed from above, the back of the hand and the pad of the thumb should both meet the wrist at the same angle so that they form the shape of the letter Y. The side view of the grip should show the end of the thumb over the top of the fore-finger, and the wrist should be dropped slightly so that the weight of the bow will not be applied to the web of skin be-tween the thumb and forefinger, but will be taken up by the pad of the thumb, as you can see in PLATES 5 and 6. Once you have got this grip correctly take care not to alter it during the rest of the shot. Many beginners tend to turn their wrist out in order to avoid the slap of the string, as in PLATE 7, but this grip is incorrect, and it actually increases the chances of the string hitting the arm.

The way you nock an arrow on the string is not an im-portant part of shooting, but it is worth getting it right and

1. Finding the correct length of arrow

2. Rosemary Thacker demonstrates the correct full-draw position

3. Another view of full-draw position. Note the extra long arrow for safety

4. Stringing the bow

learning how to do it almost without thinking so that you will avoid unnecessary fumbling, which could spoil your concentration. Without altering your grip, bring the bow up to waist height and hold it parallel to the ground. See PLATE 8. With your right hand take an arrow from your quiver by the nock, bring it over the bow and lay it across the bow on the arrow-rest. You will see that one of the three feathers is a different colour to the other two, and turn the arrow until this one, the 'cock-feather', is uppermost, away from the bow. Now push the arrow on to the nocking-point which you fitted earlier. At this point most beginners take hold of the arrow with their left forefinger, but avoid the temptation; if you have made the nocking-point correctly the arrow will stay there.

As I mentioned earlier, the string is pulled back with the first three fingers of the right hand, so place your forefinger on the string above the arrow and the second and third fingers together on the string below the arrow. The tab will be between the fingers and the string, and the slot in the tab will allow the nock to lie between the first two fingers. Take the string in the first crease of the fingers, and make sure that the third finger is well on, for this one tends to be a lazy one. The middle finger should not touch the arrow; there should be a gap of an eighth of an inch between them, but no more. Pull back the string for an inch or two, and see that the back of the hand, the wrist, and the forearm are all in a straight line. It is particularly important that the knuckles are flat. See PLATE 9.

When you are quite happy that everything is correct, stand up straight and look at the target. Start to push the left hand forward whilst you lift the right hand towards the chin, bringing the bow upright at the same time. During this drawing action it is important to keep your gaze on the target and not on the equipment. Try your hardest to keep your body still, for the draw should be done only by the arms and shoulders. At the end of the draw the bow should be perfectly upright, and as your right hand reaches the end of the draw it should slide underneath the chin until the string reaches the centre of the chin. This relationship of the hand and string to the chin is called the 'anchor'.

During the draw, many beginners find that as they get the

string half-way back the arrow suddenly falls off the arrow-rest or else it swings out sideways. The reason for this is that as they feel the pull increasing they think that they must curl their fingers more to stop the string slipping off, and this extra curl is imparted to the arrow, which then swings away from the bow. The remedy is to make sure before you draw up that the fingers are sufficiently on the string at the beginning to make it unnecessary to curl them more during the draw. If you still have trouble, draw up slowly, watch the fingers very carefully, and you will be able to see them start to curl more as the weight comes on. Practise this a few times whilst watching the fingers, and when you have cured the trouble go back to watching the target during the draw.

The position of the anchor at the end of the draw is most important, and this can be practised many times in front of a mirror, both face on and sideways. Any time spent on getting the anchor right will amply repay itself during shooting. The string should be pulled back hard into the centre of the chin and the forefinger should be pressed tightly against the underside of the chin, with no gap showing. The thumb will be tucked down against the neck and the little finger should hang loosely and not be curled into the palm. See PLATE 2 again.

Now let us have a look at the arm holding the bow. This should not be absolutely rigid, for this will cause the elbow to be in the path of the string, with painful results. Instead, hold the bow-arm very slightly bent, not much, but with the elbow just out of lock. Both shoulders should be dropped, as though you are trying to stand as tall as possible. This is one of the reasons why you should learn to shoot with a light-weight bow, for archers who have commenced shooting using a heavy bow invariably have a raised left shoulder and shoot in a hunched position.

This then is the basic position used in modern target archery to give the greatest accuracy, and you must draw and anchor time and time again until you can go straight into the correct position. Don't be tempted to rush this part of shooting, for no matter how carefully and accurately you learn to aim, which is the next step, it will be wasted without a good anchor.

Whenever you are shooting, no matter what the distance, the aiming eye should always be focussed on the target, not the bowsight. A good distance at which to start shooting is twenty yards, so put a mark on the ground twenty yards from the target and stand astride it. Archery is different from many sports in that we have one foot on either side of the distance line rather than standing behind it.

Take a rough measure of the distance between your right eye and the underside of your chin, and then put your pin on the top limb of the bow at this height above the arrow-rest. Without drawing, hold the bow upright and adjust the pin so that you can see about one quarter of an inch of it sticking out from the side of the bow.

Get your feet into the correct position, nock an arrow, carefully take your grip on the string, and come to full draw, paying particular attention to your anchor. Move the bow so that the head of the pin is right on the centre of the target. If you are focussing on the target the pin will be slightly blurred. Now close the left eye. If the pin is still on the centre of the target, the right eye, which you are using for aiming, is the controlling eye and will take charge of the aiming even if you shoot with both eyes open. If when you shut your left eye the pin suddenly appeared a long way off to the left of the target, it means that your left eye is your controlling eye, and will therefore have to be kept closed during aiming. The only other choice in this case is to change everything over and to learn to shoot left-handed. In an earlier book I suggested that before deciding which hand to hold the bow in, the archer should discover which is his controlling eye, but having taught a fair number of beginners since then I am now of the opinion that it is easier to learn to shoot with one eye shut than it is with the bow in the wrong hand. Beginners usually have a definite preference for holding the bow in a particular hand and feel awkward the other way.

During the period of aiming you must try to get the pin as steady as you can on the centre of the target, but at the same time you must try to keep a good anchor. When you are happy with your aim, loose the arrow by throwing open all your three fingers at once, and pulling the hand back slightly.

Don't move your body, but keep quite still until your arrow
has struck. On a few occasions I have come across people who
were unable to let the arrow go at all, but simply stood there
opening and closing one finger at a time and saying helplessly,
'It won't go, it won't go!' They probably didn't realize it
themselves, but they were simply frightened of what was going
to happen when all the weight was suddenly released. If this
should happen to you, the cure is quite simple. Hold the bow
horizontally and pull the string back for a short distance, no
more than two or three inches, with the arrow pointing at the
ground. With this minimum amount of pull and with the
string well away from the face it is easy to let the string go,
and by doing this several times, increasing the draw slightly
each time, you find that it will cure the trouble at full draw
with a good anchor.

The position on the bow at which you placed the pin was
chosen very approximately, so it will probably be necessary to
alter this early on in your shooting. If you are getting a good
anchor you will find after several arrows that they are landing
not too far from each other, even if this is nowhere near the
target! When they are beginning to group like this it is possible to get them to hit the target by altering the position of
the sight. If the arrows are all going over the top of the target,
then raise the sight; underneath, then lower the sight. If they
go to the left of the target, then move the sight to the left by
pulling it away from the bow a little; to the right, then push
the sight in a little. Try to remember the rule that when altering the sight always follow the arrows with the sight, not the
opposite. If you think about it, you will realize that when
the arrows are going to the left, by moving the sight to the
left you are automatically moving the bow to the right, and
this will bring the arrows over. There is no point in altering
the sight after each arrow; it is the position of the whole group
which is important. The groups your arrows make will be very
large at first, but as you practise what you have learned and
try to get closer and closer to the method outlined in this
chapter you will find that more and more of your shots land
in the centre of the target.

The next four chapters should be treated with caution by

newcomers. They start right again at the beginning of shooting an arrow, but they go into much greater detail over every point of style. If you are a beginner, stay with the present chapter, for it contains more than enough for you to remember. When you have had several days' shooting you can read on, for then you will understand all the points made, and they won't confuse you.

5. *The Draw*

The style used for modern archery began to evolve in Victorian days, and looks very little like the method used by mediaeval archers. The biggest advance towards greater accuracy appears to have been made by Horace Ford, who invented the anchor under the chin and made record scores with this method. Since then shooting has been studied and refined by leading archers and coaches, until we have reached the style of today, which is producing the highest scores ever seen. The search has been for a style which could be reproduced the same for every shot, for when arrows can be loosed with exactly the same thrust at exactly the same angle they will land in exactly the same spot. Because people are not all made to precisely the same proportions you will find that not even the best archers shoot the same in every detail, but you will find that they are all trying to remove any part of their shooting technique that cannot be repeated every time. The better tournament arrows made today are so alike within the set that no archer coud tell the difference between them, so when all the arrows do not hit the Gold it is entirely due to variations in the archer's method of shooting them.

It is often said in archery that one must teach the correct way and not show or mention the wrong way, but many archers who think that they are shooting properly have one or two really damaging faults in their shooting which are holding them back. When their faults are demonstrated to them they can see what their trouble is and so work on it to improve their scores. These four chapters will therefore not only discuss refinements of good technique, but will also try to show the bad points, so that all the archers who have been shooting for a long time but have never made Master Bowman or even First Class may be able to spot their own troubles and so improve. Much of my information has been gleaned from the various evening classes I have taught over the years, but my present class for Advanced Archery is the one which has been the most helpful to me in the writing of this book. The class is made up of archers who are active members of their clubs and their standard of shooting ranges from Third to First Class. Because they are experienced archers and not absolute beginners the faults they have are typical of archers everywhere and are ideal for study in order to help others. Some of the better archers have faults so small that they are very difficult to detect, and obviously it is true to say that the better you are the more difficult it is to improve further.

Let us go back right to the beginning when you first go up to the shooting line. So many archers simply stand astride the line and immediately reach for an arrow. The better archers take their time over it, looking down at their feet and lining them up with the target, shuffling about and adjusting their position until they are satisfied, like a champion golfer about to take a long putt. When they have found the right position, they shoot all three arrows without moving their feet.

It is not possible to say what is the right distance between the feet, for people's bodies vary so much in size and proportions that the most comfortable distance must vary from one person to another. Having the feet apart does help to brace the body against the wind, so choose the gap which is most natural to you, and then try not to vary it. Now move the knees back so that they lock, for this will give you even more protection against the wind. I know of a few archers who now tighten the muscles of their knees so that their kneecaps move up slightly and make the legs more rigid, but I would not recommend this, for keeping the muscles of the knees tight all through the shot does need a conscious effort of will which can ill be spared during the anchoring and aiming. During these latter two parts of shooting you really need every bit of concentration, and there is simply not enough to spare to keep the knees tight all the time. So locking the knees backwards is enough.

The grip on the bow is determined to a great extent by the shaping of the bow handle, especially with composite bows, for

the makers of these all put a great deal of care into the shaping
of the handle to make it a comfortable fit when it is held in the
right position. It is certain that the nearer to the arrow-rest
the weight of the bow can be supported the better the bow will
shoot, so modern handles are shaped to throw the weight well
up. To keep the weight near the arrow and to avoid any backward pressure from the fingers on the bottom of the handle
most good archers now use an open grip, with only the forefinger holding the bow, and all the others being open. In
addition to bringing the weight of the bow up the handle, this
looser grip also gives the archer a feeling of delicacy and precision which reduces the wavering in the bow arm. Some
archers shoot with all the fingers of the bow hand open so
that the arm is acting as a mere prop for the bow, but these
archers must use a strap to hold the bow to their wrist, otherwise they will have to grab the bow as they loose to avoid
dropping it, and this last-second grab will destroy the accuracy
of the shot. If you are using an open grip, will you make sure
the next time you shoot that you are not grabbing the bow?

The wrist should be in a central position so that the weight
of the bow will be taken directly down the arm. If the wrist is
held either in or out of this line then extra effort will have to
be expended to stop the wrist being twisted even more, and at
the loose the bow will be jerked in the direction the wrist is
facing. Study PLATES 5, 6 and 7 and compare them with your
own. People who are using self-wood or solid glass-fibre bows
should be particularly careful over their grip on the bow, and
should ensure that their forefinger is not protruding above the
arrow-rest and so lifting the pile of the arrow.

In Chapter 4 you learned a method of nocking an arrow on
the string. Remember that the cock feather must point away
from the bow, and the nock should fit snugly on the string,
neither too tight nor too loose. Many archers today use arrows
with four fletchings instead of three, so that there is no cock-
feather, but the archer should still use one side of his arrows
as the cock-feather side, otherwise any slight bends that may
appear through damage will be doubled in their effect by
shooting the arrow first one way round and then the other.

The position of the three drawing fingers on the string is

most important. You already know that one goes above the arrow and two go underneath, but exactly where should they be in relation to the arrow? Before the bow is drawn the string is a straight line, but as it is drawn it becomes an angle with the arrow at the apex. This means that the string will press on either side of the drawing fingers and this pressure will cause the fingers to 'pinch' the arrow and so spoil the loose. To counteract this, archers leave a gap of an eighth of an inch under the arrow, between the nock and the middle finger, when they place their fingers on the string. The fingers will still touch the arrow at full draw, but it will just be a gentle contact and no more. You might say why not have a gap either side of the arrow instead of only underneath, but by introducing a gap between the arrow and the forefinger you are introducing a variable which can never be made the same each time, and it is most important that the distance between the aiming eye and the nock *is* the same every time.

It is important that the gap is maintained beneath the arrow, but no more than an eighth of an inch, and it must be judged accurately for every shot. The archer who has a good central group, but continually gets one or two arrows extremely high should suspect that he has forgotten to keep this gap, for pinching tends to lift the arrow from the rest. Many times I have seen archers taking most careful aim, completely unaware that their arrow has risen an inch or more above the rest, and is pointing well above the target. Be careful not to let this gap get too large, for I have seen archers drawing with more than an inch gap between the middle finger and the nock.

There have been lots of different opinions over the years over how much of the fingers should be on the string, but the general opinion today is to get the string in the first crease of all three fingers. Because the middle finger is usually longer than the other two it may be necessary to bend this one a little more, but do make sure that the third finger is well on. The fingers should be squarely on the string, not sloping down, and if you make sure that the third finger has the string in its first crease it will help to ensure that the fingers are not sloping. When an archer takes hold of the string with sloping fingers he will come up into an anchor with the back of his hand tilted up and this will make it difficult for him to get the forefinger properly under his chin.

Now take up just a little weight of the bow. Only the first joints of the fingers should bend and it is particularly important that the back of the hand is flat and in a straight line with the wrist and arm, see PLATE 9. For every single shot throughout your shooting career you should spend at least five seconds getting your fingers correctly on the string, before starting to draw. If you watch archers at a tournament and note those who simply grab the string and come straight into the anchor, you will find that not one of them will reach the top ten places. When you are quite satisfied with the position of the hand on the string, take a look at the little finger. This should be completely loose and relaxed. If you attempt to curl it into your palm you will find that it forces the knuckles where the fingers join the hand to jut out, and this will spoil that nice flat hand.

Before starting to draw, stand erect, and face the target. From this moment until the arrow has been loosed and struck the target the gaze should not leave the gold. Never look at the drawing-hand or the arrow during the draw. The only exception to this is when you suspect something wrong in your manner of drawing or anchoring, and then you may need to look down to check yourself, but for your normal shooting it must be the Gold.

The drawing of the bow should be shared by both arms, the left one pushing the bow towards the target whilst the right pulls back towards the chin. The bow is brought into the vertical position at the same time. Some archers, including some very good ones, extend the left arm first and then draw back with the right, but to do this it is necessary to swing the right shoulder forward before the draw and then pull it back again during the draw. Again, it is not uncommon to see archers lift the bow almost directly above their heads before drawing in a sort of downwards swoop, but this is just wasted effort that might be needed later in the competition. It certainly adds nothing to the accuracy of the shot.

Only the arms should move during the draw with no backwards or forward movement of the body. So many archers who are trying to get a good anchor on the chin move their head forward or even bend forward from the waist in order to get the head nearer to the string, but instead of moving their chin towards the string they should really keep their head and body still and pull the string into the chin with their arms. The draw can be practised in front of a mirror, but it is better to get a friend to watch you who can tell you if you are moving.

6. *The Anchor*

At the end of the draw the archer's right hand should slide easily under the chin into the position we call the anchor, with the string pulled firmly into the centre of the chin. Let us stop and consider for a moment why this anchor is so important. The distance a bow will throw an arrow is determined by the amount the string is drawn back, so obviously if the string is drawn back a different amount each time it will impart a different amount of energy to each arrow, causing them one moment to hit the top of the target, the next moment the bottom. When the string is pulled hard into the chin, the chin is acting as a backstop and is ensuring that the string is drawn back the same amount every time. See PLATES 10 and 11. This is only true when the string is in the centre of the chin. If the draw is made to the side of the chin it can be pulled farther back without the archer realizing he is doing it. Similarly if the archer lets the string away from his chin by the merest fraction of an inch, the arrows will start to drop below the centre of the target.

Now let us consider why the forefinger must be underneath the chin and pressed against it. For all the arrows to fall in one place they must be loosed at the same angle each time as well as having the same amount of thrust, but although bows have a foresight they have no backsight, so how do you get the angle the same every time? By the simple expedient of placing the forefinger against the underside of the chin you are making the distance between the aiming eye and the nock a constant one, and so the angle of the arrow will always be the same. It is a simple matter to explain this and to understand it, but many archers find it very difficult to do. So many archers leave a gap between the forefinger and the chin which makes the arrows shoot high, whilst others let their forefinger gradually rise up the side of the chin, which makes the arrows drop, but neither of these two types realize that they are doing it. A further difficulty is encountered if the archer forgets to keep the back of his hand flat, for when it is curved it is impossible to keep the forefinger under the chin and the string in the centre at one and the same time.

A point that is often overlooked is the need to keep the teeth closed during the anchor. Can you think why? When the teeth are apart the gap between them will be added on to the distance between the aiming eye and the nock of the arrow, so once more the arrows will start to go high. I do not mean that the front teeth should be clenched together, but the mouth should be in the normal closed position with the upper front teeth a little ahead of the bottom.

During the anchor the thumb will be held loosely against the neck, but should not be deliberately curled tight. Similarly, the little finger should be completely relaxed and hanging loose, never curled into the palm of the hand. If you curl it into your palm it will raise the knuckles on the back of the hand which will give you a bad anchor and a bad loose. This advice to make sure the back of the hand is flat cannot be stressed often enough. One should never make sweeping statements, but I will go so far as to say that if you shoot with raised knuckles you will find it extremely difficult to make First Class and you will certainly never make Master Bowman. Of course, it follows that it will be sure to hold you back on the lower classifications as well. When the back of the hand is flat the weight of the bow is taken in a straight line through the hand and along the forearm; as soon as the knuckles are raised this straight line is given a kink which will not only prevent a good loose, but will put a strain on the hand because of the additional work the muscles will have to do just to keep the hand bent in this fashion. If a day's shooting gives you pains in the hand or wrist, check these knuckles. This fault is to be seen in so many archers that I make no apology for spending so much time on it. When told of it during tuition so many archers say, 'Oh, I always shoot like this' which really means that they cannot be bothered to change it. If you find that it is part of your style, please make an effort to alter it. You will probably find that your scores go down at first, as they will after any major change in your style, but I am confident that once you have learned to keep the hand flat you will find that they reach much greater heights than before.

Now you know how to keep the angle of the arrow and the thrust behind it the same for every shot, so why not learn to keep the angle of the head the same each time as well? This is easily done by placing the tip of the nose against the string during the anchor, but remember, it is not a substitute for the chin anchor, it is an additional check. Some archers also purse their lips to kiss the string during the anchor, but this is not a habit to encourage. It doesn't harm your shooting until you reach the stage where it once more becomes a substitute for a good anchor on the chin. If you pull the string hard into your chin and then kiss the string it is fine, but if you are kissing the string with it well away from your chin, what are you achieving? The lips can be pushed forward from the face for half an inch or more, and this is what you will lose on your draw length.

Remember that a good anchor is obtained by pulling the drawing hand back under the chin, and not by pushing the head forward to meet it. It is perfectly acceptable to lift the head a little as the drawing hand comes back if by dropping the chin on to the forefinger you can get a more correct anchor; touching the nose on the string then gives you your check on the angle of the head. People who are a bit on the plump side with the makings of a double chin may find they are letting flesh under the chin roll forward and are anchoring against this instead of pulling the string hard against the bone.

Occasionally an archer will be under the impression that his forefinger is pressed hard against his chin, while all the time it is his tab instead. Do make sure that your tab is trimmed down to below the outside edge of the first finger so that it will not come between this finger and the chin. The traditional tab has holes to take the first and third fingers as in Fig. 2a, but a recent idea is the tab shown in Fig. 2b (see page 24). This has holes for the second and third fingers, leaving the first finger free, and this does make for a better anchor, although it may still be necessary to trim a little off before use.

Shooting-gloves are used by many archers, including some very expert ones, but they are a potential source of great troubles for the unwary. I have written at some length on the need to keep the back of the hand flat with just the first joint holding the string, but some makes of gloves are so stiff in the fingers that it is impossible to bend the fingers at all except where they join the hand! Any beginner who is unfortunate enough to buy one of these gloves at the beginning of his shooting will develop a terrible anchor. Even if he changes to a tab later on it will be extremely difficult for him to learn to shoot with a flat hand after months or years with one of these gloves. The only gloves that are of any use are those made from very soft kid, with another layer of soft leather sewn on the pads of the finger-tips, but even these encourage pinching. When an archer pinches with a tab his fingers gets sore, so he makes sure to leave that important gap, and the pinching stops. If he is using a glove, the pinching rubs on the glove, not the skin, so the archer does not find out that he is pinching. When you see a top archer using a glove, you can be sure that he is aware of these dangers and is taking care to avoid them.

Although a few archers use just two fingers to draw instead of three, it does need very strong fingers to do this successfully, and I am convinced that three fingers are needed to give the sort of firm control that is required for really high scores. The first and third fingers are usually similar in length whilst the middle finger is longer, so that when three fingers are used the part of the string which takes the arrow will be vertical at full draw, rather than sloping. I have already mentioned that the third finger can be a lazy one, but sometimes an archer will neglect to keep the forefinger curled around the string, and this is often the cause of 'mis-nocking'. This is the name given to what happens when the string is loosed but the arrow just clatters to the ground instead of being shot. This can be caused by the nocking-point being too tight or too loose, but it can also be caused by anchoring with the fore-finger straight. When the string is not held back by this finger it will slope forward at the nocking-point so that the nock of the arrow will have no support underneath it. In this position it takes only the slightest movement for the nock to fall off, but the archer will not know that this has happened until he looses.

Sometimes archers who have long ago got over the troubles of the arrow coming off the rest during the draw suddenly go through a spell of the same trouble when they are perfecting their anchor. This usually happens because they are so keen to get the string back hard into the chin that they curl the tips of the fingers just a little more to increase the pressure and this pushes the arrow off, whereas they should pull the whole hand and arm back just a little more instead.

If the arrow drops off the rest at full draw and you are able to put it back on with the drawing fingers, then you are starting the draw with the fingers too close to the arrow and you are pinching.

While you are mentally checking over all the points in your anchor you must not forget your bow arm. If you are sure that you are getting a really good anchor and loose on every shot, but your arrows are dropping to the bottom of the target, then it is probably because your bow arm is beginning to collapse under the weight. A friend can check this easily enough for you by watching the tip of your arrow from the side and seeing if it slowly moves forward from the bow while you are aiming; this is called creeping. Another method of discovering if this is happening is to fit a draw-check, as described in Chapter 10.

Keeping the bow-arm at just the right stretch is an important part of shooting. The bow is so eager to push you down that you must keep up the pressure with your left arm. Beginners have a tendency to hunch the left shoulder and lock the elbow in order to cope with this pressure, but this is wrong and is one of the reasons why you should start with a light bow. If you try to push a little harder towards the target during aiming you will be keeping the bow at its proper draw.

When you are drawing your bow, most of the effort will be done by the muscles of the upper arm, but when you have reached full draw and have got a good anchor you should take some of the weight away from the arm and put it onto the shoulder blades. This is called the Second Hold. The shoulder blades are drawn together and your chest is pushed out so that you feel as though you are going inside the bow. This action will bring the drawing arm more behind the arrow and will help to make you more steady, as well as giving a better loose. This is one of those things that can be practised indoors without shooting. Come up in front of a mirror and get a good anchor, then try to push your chest forward so that you can see the elbow of your drawing arm come more behind the arrow, but take care that the string does not come out of the centre of the chin.

The position of the elbow during the anchor is quite important. If you look at archers at full draw you will see that the elbow is held fairly high. The pressure of the bow arm is not applied at the arrow-rest, but two or three inches below this, on the handle, and the drawing arm must oppose this pressure in a straight line, not at an angle. So if you were to draw a straight line from the tip of the elbow to the nock of the arrow and then extend it on, you would find that it passes not through the pile of the arrow, but through the handle.

Beginners generally give far too little attention to their anchor. They tend to just pull the string back to somewhere on their face and straight away start aiming at the target. The anchor should be completed first, and then the archer must check over in his mind that everything is perfect before starting to aim. Even during the aiming the archer must keep his anchor in mind, otherwise the string will gradually come out of the chin and the bow-arm will slowly let down.

7. *Aiming*

Before going into the various ways of aiming I would like to explain something which affects aiming considerably but which is often confusing to beginners; the meaning of 'spine'. This is simply a method of indicating how stiff an arrow is. If an arrow is supported at the nock and the pile and then a weight of one and a quarter pounds is placed in the middle the arrow will bend by a certain amount. The distance the arrow moves out of the straight is measured in hundredths of an inch, and this is the spine value for this particular shaft. To make this perfectly clear, let us take an arrow and measure the deflection. If it goes down 65/100ths, then the arrow is 65 spine. Simple, isn't it? Obviously, the lower the number, the stiffer the arrow. You need not remember how the spine is determined, but it is worthwhile remembering that 60 is an average, so 53 is a stiff arrow and 65 is whippy.

The reason that archers need some method of determining the stiffness of an arrow is that efficient or heavy bows shoot better with a stiff arrow, while weak or slow bows need a whippier one. If at some time in your shooting career you decide you would do better with shorter arrows it is often better to part-exchange them for a new set of the correct spine for your bow, than to get the old ones shortened, for this would make them stiffer at the rate of approximately seven units of spine for every inch.

There is no need for you to worry about this question of spine for manufacturers and retailers will always supply arrows of the right spine when you tell them the make of your bow and what its weight is.

Now we will get back to aiming, and you will see how spine affects it.

In your early attempts at shooting you will have to give

so much attention to keeping your anchor in place, your bow-arm straight, and all the other things you have to think about, that all you could be expected to do in aiming is to get the pin in the centre of the target before loosing. In Chapter 4, I said that when the arrows are grouping away from the Gold you must follow the group with the sight, which will have the effect of moving the bow in the opposite direction. In spite of this your arrows will still vary from side to side, the amount of this depending to some extent on how good your anchor is, so we have got to bring the string into your sighting.

To explain this with an extreme example, imagine that your sight is on the Gold but the string is to the right of your chin. Because you have taken the nock to the right the arrow will fly to the left. Now imagine that the sight is again on the Gold, but now the string is on the left of the chin. The arrow will now fly to the right. The point to note in this is that the arrows went in different directions even though the sight was on the Gold on both occasions.

Getting the string in the centre of the chin each time does a great deal towards cutting down this variation, but because you cannot judge the amount you have turned the head towards the target for each shot you have to note where the string is in your sighting. When you can see that the string is in the same place while you are aiming, you will know that the nock of the arrow is in the same side-to-side relationship to the sight.

Now let us see where this string should be. First of all let me repeat what I said earlier, that only the target should be in focus, so the string, which is very close to the eye, will appear as a vague blur.

Most archers place this blur on the limb of the bow so that it touches the edge of the bow, with the sight visible protruding from the limb. On no account should you look through the gap between the string and the bow because this gap can never be judged the same each time and the variation will show in poorer groups. The left hand edge of the string-blur should be made to coincide with the left hand edge of the bow.

Generally speaking, a whippy arrow will fly to the right and a stiff one to the left, so it could happen that your arrows shoot to the right with your string in this position and that the place they strike the target is covered by your bow. To get your arrows in the Gold you are having to aim to the left of it and so your bow is covering the Gold which you cannot see at all. If your bowsight is only just protruding you cannot move it to the right or it will disappear altogether, so one answer is to move the bowstring to the right; this will then bring the arrows to the left. However, just moving the blur an indeterminate amount to the right will not do. To place the bowstring in the same place every time you must paint a line or apply a narrow length of sticky tape vertically on the bow limb and this will take the place of the edge of your bow when you are aiming. A better method, but one that is not always practicable is to pack the edge of the bow out at the arrow rest with layers of leather or plastic. This packing will move the pile of the arrow a little to the left and therefore the arrows will shoot more to the left. Don't use the sort of surgical tape which is used for dressing minor wounds, for this exerts a lot of drag on the arrow. Whichever method you decide on, it must become a regular part of your aiming, and not changed from day to day.

If with the sight just protruding your arrows group to the left, you have no problem, just move the sight out a short distance. You are much better off with a certain amount of bowsight out, for if you have to shoot in a wind coming from the left it will carry your arrows over and you will have a bit of leeway on your sight so that you can move it to the right without it disappearing behind the limb.

Another method of aiming is used by some archers when their arrows shoot a long way over to the left. Instead of placing the bowstring on the edge of the bow they bring it over to the left until it is in line with the sight. They don't shoot through the gap between the string and the bow known as the bow-window, but they line the left hand edge of this string blur up with the sight and Gold. In theory it should be easier to get the Gold, the pin, and the string in one straight line than to line up the pin on the Gold and then the string on the edge of the bow, for in the latter case you are trying to look in two slightly different directions at once. However, if not too much of the pin is showing it is not too difficult to concentrate on getting the pin on the Gold and still be aware of the string on the edge of the limb without it taking up too much of your attention.

When you are aiming at long distances you must try very hard to get your sight on the Gold rather than just on the target, and at shorter distances the Gold is too big and you must aim at the centre of it. You have to learn to stand as steady as possible, for you will get nowhere if you loose when your sight is wavering about all over the target. If you loose when your sight has passed the Gold and is on the Blue, you mustn't be surprised if your arrow lands in the Blue. It will steady you if you hold your breath during the aim. Take a deep breath as you draw, let half of it out as you anchor, then hold it until you have loosed.

When you get your aim as steady as you are able you must pause on the aim before loosing, and this pause is most important. If you loose as soon as your sight comes to rest on the Gold without giving this pause you will eventually get to the state where you loose automatically as soon as you see your sight on the Gold. This happens quite involuntarily, the arrow just goes.

This peculiar condition is called target shyness, and it sometimes takes a different form where the archer doesn't loose when he gets his sight on the Gold, but he just cannot get his sight to move on to the Gold at all no matter how hard he tries. Sometimes they are 'triggered' into shooting before they are ready. My wife went through a very bad patch in her shooting when just touching the string to her chin was enough to send the arrow on its way, and this had been caused by her aiming during the draw instead of drawing and anchoring before even thinking about aiming.

It can take a long time and a lot of perseverance to cure target shyness, but the important thing to remember is that the pause between aiming and loosing must be brought back into the archer's style. Changing to a lighter bow for a while is a help, for this will make it easier to get a really solid anchor.

Repeatedly drawing up and aiming without any intention of loosing will help, and when the archer has done this for a while with a light bow he can hold the aim for some time and can decide during the aim whether to loose or not. I am sure that given the time and the will it can be cured. Now and again one meets an archer who talks for so long about his target shyness that one tends to think that perhaps he prefers the disease to the cure.

8. The Loose

This is probably the most important part of shooting, for even if everything else is perfect a bad loose will completely ruin all the care and attention that has gone into the shot. If I could point to just one point about a good loose, I would say that the most important thing is that it is a backward loose. If the string is pulled hard into the chin so that it can go back no further, then just a little more backwards pressure on the drawing arm will pull the string off the finger tips. Make sure that the extra pressure to give a good loose is not done by bending the fingers in a sort of harp plucking action; the whole forearm must come back so that the string is forced off the finger tips. If you have a good second hold you will feel your shoulder blades come closer together.

At the same time as this is happening the bow-hand must be exerting pressure towards the Gold. This is important because it will stop you from loosing when you are under-drawn, and it will also help to stop you from swinging your arm away from the target in any direction.

In a good loose not only does the hand come backwards, but it comes backwards in a straight line with the arrow. If, after the loose, your hand has come back two or three inches but is in a straight line behind its original position you have got it right, but get a friend to check you, for you may be cheating without realizing it. By this I mean that I have seen archers with really poor looses who immediately place their hand on their neck underneath their ear and then think that they have managed a good backward loose.

The difficulty with checking on and practising your loose is that you cannot see what you yourself are doing; you can only go by what you feel is happening. Never take your loose for granted; because you checked once that you have got a good loose does not mean that you will still have the same loose six months later.

A common fault with beginners is that they sometimes develop a forward loose. They get a good anchor, aim very carefully, but then just as they loose, their drawing-hand suddenly goes forward by about six inches and they loose from there. It does of course occur very quickly, but the whole hand is thrown forward before the string is finally let go. It is surprising that this fault is so common, because to do it the archer has to suddenly reverse the direction in which he is pulling. It is probably caused by fear of the power of the bow and a desire to get the string away from the face before it is loosed. This is borne out by the fact that most archers with this type of loose also flinch at the same time. Because the arrow is not given its full draw length; it is after all being loosed six inches forward of the face; it will have only a portion of the total available thrust, so it will always drop short. I remember one lady shooting on my target in a tournament asking me to have a look at her bow to see if it was faulty in any way because her marks were dropping rapidly end by end. Of course it was nothing to do with her bow, it was her loose that was deteriorating. Once experienced archers realize they are doing this it is a simple matter to correct it, but for newcomers it can be a problem. One way to tackle it is to stress that in the loose, the backwards pull of the drawing arm should tear the string off the fingers rather than the fingers just opening and letting the string go. A flinch that the archer has had for some time is much more difficult to cure, as are most faults that have become part of the archer's style over a long period of time. A flinch can eventually be overcome by concentrating on pushing the bow towards the Gold and by forcing oneself to keep the eyes open throughout the loose; not only open, but staring at the Gold. Here again it is a great help to have a friend to watch who can give you encouraging progress reports.

The most common form of loose is probably the one which archers call a 'dead' loose. The hand does not move forward, but the fingers just open to let the string go, with no backward movement at all. This will give satisfactory scores up to a point, but the archer using it will probably not be able to get much further than Second Class. The marks on his bow will be reasonably consistent, but lower than he would expect with his particular draw weight. When you first become aware that your loose is not as good as it might be it is better to practise with no thought for your score than to try to improve it during a Round. The act of loosing is over so quickly that it is difficult to feel exactly what is happening, which is why it is better to concentrate on what your loose feels like and ignore where the arrow goes. Try shooting at a boss without a face on from about ten yards, perhaps even with your eyes shut, and then you will really be able to find out what you are doing. I thought that I had a marvellous loose (all coaches do) until a member of my evening class, who was supposed to be getting help from me, told me that my loose was dead, and that my fingers were finishing up on the front of my throat. I had shot for months with the sort of harp-plucking action that would have got me a good place in any celestial orchestra, but was certainly not getting me good scores. So please don't take your loose for granted; it may be a lot worse than when you last gave it some attention.

Sometimes you will see archers loose and finish up with their hand either on their chest or well out to the side of their face. The hand should always come straight back from the arrow, although the amount it does so will vary from one archer to another. There should be no sideways variation.

When the arrow has left your finger-tips it is not the finish of the shot; not if you want to get good scores, it isn't. The follow-through is important for accurate shooting, and you can check this for yourself at any tournament. Watch the archers shooting, and you will find that those who drop their bow-arm and their drawing-hand the moment they have loosed are never among the leaders. When you loose only two things should move; your drawing-hand should come back a little and your bow-hand should push towards the target. Note that I said towards the target, not up or down or sideways. Apart from these small movements you should be motionless, and you should keep in this position for at least three seconds. There are two reasons for this pause after loosing and the first of these is that any movement you make after loosing will eventually become part of your style and will happen *as* you loose and not after, and this will deflect your arrow. It may deflect it by a very tiny amount, but remember that the line between the Gold and the Red is also a very thin line. The second reason for the pause is that it enables you to think about the shot and analyse why it was a good shot or why it was poor. You can see if your bow hand has jumped out of line with the target and you can feel if your drawing-hand is in the right place. When you make a habit of coming down immediately after loosing you are deliberately throwing away an excellent chance of checking on your style.

It is a great temptation to look up to follow the flight of the arrow after the loose, but do try to school yourself into keeping your gaze firmly on the Gold. Once the arrow has left you there is nothing you can do to make it change its course, more's the pity, so keep looking at the centre of the target. It is true that at the longer distances you can frequently get a much better idea of where they are striking the target if you watch their flight, but this is overshadowed by the disadvantages. Flicking the eyes up to watch the arrow usually spoils the follow-through because the archer no longer sees where his bow is after the shot, and he may in fact be moving the bow out of the way in order to see his arrow better. When you stare at the Gold after the loose you will be building up that determination to hit it and you will be more readily aware of any unnecessary movement that is giving you a poor follow-through. It is so difficult *not* to watch the arrow that I should think that about ninety per cent of all archers do it, but the remaining ten per cent includes the champions.

I have several times mentioned that it is helpful to watch good archers at a tournament to pick up tips that will help you to improve your own shooting, so it is only fair to tell you that you will see some of our most expert archers doing things that seem entirely wrong according to what I have already written. For instance, some of them not only have a backwards loose, but their whole drawing-arm opens out, while others swing their bows well away from the direction of the target when they loose. These archers have got to the top by continually studying their own styles and have found methods of improving their scores by variations of techniques which would confuse or hold back lesser mortals. When their bow-arms swing away from the target they are not only aware of it, but they know why they are doing it and exactly by how much they are doing it. If you watch them very closely you will see that the first part of the swing is *towards* the target and the sideways movement is merely the finish of an excellent follow-through. Similarly, when the archer's drawing-arm opens right out at the end of the loose, this is merely the follow-through to a superb backwards loose. If you as a newcomer try to copy one of the country's leading archers with a style peculiar to him, you may eventually look like him, but you will not get scores like him, because he has the self-knowledge gained over many years of shooting, and you haven't.

Most of these variations from the modern target archery style are derived from America, and they do help very good archers to get even better, but do wait until you have reached a First Class standard with the method set out in this book before you risk losing your good scores by playing with your style.

9. *The will to win*

It is not necessary to be a champion to derive pleasure from shooting with a bow, for there are many enjoyable things about the sport and the satisfaction of a good score is only one of them. Some people simply enjoy the companionship of their fellow archers, while others treat it as a quiet day's relaxation in the open air. Some archers get satisfaction from participating in a skill that has its origins hidden in his country's past, while newcomers may get all they want from the sport from the simple fun in shooting arrows no matter where they strike. I can remember from my own early days how much fun it was just to loose and watch my arrows whistle through the air towards the target. But there can be no denying that if you do something at all, then it is more satisfying to do it well. This is not intended to belittle those who shoot for years and never achieve very much in the way of good scores, for I have no doubt that they enjoy their shooting, but I want to try to convey to newcomers how important it is to approach their new sport with the right attitude of mind if they are to do well.

People who have been thinking about taking up archery have often asked me 'Do you think that I might make a good archer?' as though a quick run over their arms and legs with a tape measure and two minutes with a slide rule would give me the answer, but of course, it doesn't work like that. Although a certain minimum physical ability is necessary, I have often been at tournament prize-givings where a thin little man has gone up to receive the first prize, to be followed by a big husky he-man who has come second, so we can be quite sure that the size and strength of one's body is not all the answer. Skill in shooting comes not from an archer's muscles, but from his mental attitude towards his archery and just how determined he is to do well at it.

This is just as true for a newcomer as it is for an expert. If when you first start shooting you feel that this is the sport for you then you must realize that your attitude towards your shooting will determine how quickly you will improve. This mental attitude depends on your own will-power, and consists of two essential aspects which have to be encouraged and developed: the ability to look inwards on yourself, and the determination to concentrate on getting things right. A new archer must be continually studying every part of his own style to get it nearer and nearer to one that can be repeated every time in exactly the same way. Archery is a very logical sport; whenever you alter any detail in your style the result of this will show itself in the place your arrow strikes, so variations in the way you shoot your arrows will cause variations in the pattern of your hits, in other words, larger groups. As your knowledge of your own way of shooting increases you can watch other archers shooting and compare their methods with your own. It won't be very long before you can see which are the better archers without seeing their scores; their styles will give it to you.

It is a mistake to confuse quantity of practice with quality. I really did know a man once who shot before he went to work, shot again when he came home, and was shooting at the club at weekends long before anyone else arrived. The fact that he could never get beyond third class was a constant source of amazement to him, but it never occurred to him that the sheer number of arrows shot was not going to improve him because he never put any thought into a single one of them. So think about how you are shooting all the time.

When you are practising, shoot slowly with a pause between each arrow. This will give you time to try to discover what went wrong with that particular arrow. Sometimes you will learn something and sometimes you won't, but do make the effort. Some archers get three arrows off in thirty seconds, and they cannot be giving real thought to what they are doing.

I can give an example of this inability to look inwards into one's own style. When it happened it came as a revelation to me, and for the first time I realized why some archers never get anywhere with their scores. I was one of several coaches

who attended a weekend course run by the GNAS for archers
who wanted to improve their shooting. The archers were
divided into groups and each group was put into the charge
of a coach who then did his best to improve their shooting.
In my group was a young lady whose shooting was so inaccurate that she would have been thrown out of a tribe of
pygmies. Her trouble was obvious; instead of a proper anchor
she was placing the wrist of her right hand against her chin
so that the string was about five inches in front of her face
and she was loosing from there. With a glaring fault like this
it didn't take long to set her on the right road, and as soon
as she was getting the string into the centre of her chin with a
good firm anchor her scoring began to leap up. At the end of
the course she went home shooting so much better and I was
very pleased to have been able to help her to make such a
noticeable improvement in her scores. This should be the
happy ending to the story, but I have to disappoint you. A
year later I went on the same course and by a coincidence
this young lady was present and placed in my group. She was
again shooting with her wrist against her chin and getting
terrible scores, and when I told her about her poor anchor
she replied 'That must be why I'm shooting so badly. Didn't
you tell me that last year?'

The moral of this story is that some archers just never bother
to think about what they are doing at all, and consequently
never get any better.

As well as trying to detect your own faults you should not
become complacent as your scores improve. No newcomer
is ever going to shoot in his first tournament and become outright winner, but he should know who his equals are and try
to beat them. When he does beat them he should study the
results sheet and find himself a higher set of equals to go
after. When you first start shooting buy a score book and a
set of handicap tables so that you can compare the different
rounds you shoot, and always try to beat your previous best
score. A high score doesn't just happen, it is made up of a lot
of good shots added together, so put the same care and attention into every arrow, as though this particular arrow was the
last one in the tournament and everything depended on it. The

only successful arrow is the one in the Gold; all the other colours are consolation prizes. Again, just because you have drawn an arrow back doesn't mean that you have got to loose it. If it doesn't feel right it is not likely to go in the Gold, so come down and try again.

The better your scores become, the more difficult it is to get further improvements, so as you improve you will have to look for smaller and smaller points of style to work on. When an archer is getting 100 points for a York Round it doesn't take much improvement in his style to get it up to 200, but when an archer is scoring 1,000 for a York it is extremely difficult to get it up to 1,010. In all this discussion on scores it is important to remember that scores are simply a reflection of an archer's style; they tell him how well his style is developing. In a tournament it is better to concentrate on your shooting, rather than on the way the figures add up. Archers who spend their time checking their arithmetic and trying to find out what score per dozen they need to reach their handicap are wasting their time. If they concentrated instead on putting all they had into each arrow the score would take care of itself.

Perhaps I can best finish this chapter on the will to win by giving you some thoughts on this subject by George Brown, who must rank as one of the greatest English archers of this century. George was British Champion in 1956 and 1960, and took second place in 1949, 1950, and 1957. He won the Southern Counties Championship in 1949, 1953 to 1958 inclusive, and again in 1960, as well as hundreds of lesser competitions. If you went to a tournament when George was at his peak and found that he was there, then you accepted that you were fighting for second place. Other archers have overtaken George since those days, but nobody has managed such a continuous succession of high scores year after year.

His first point is that it is most important for an archer to know himself and his own capabilities, which bears out what I said earlier. Then he says that a good archer must set himself a target. It is not possible to ever be satisfied, but the good archer must always be after the unattainable. This is similar to my advice to try to beat your equals, but you will notice that a champion of George's standard talks about chasing the unattainable, where a poorer shot like myself talks about beating other archers. An interesting point, there.

He lays great stress on the need for concentration. One must be able to disregard everything and everybody when on the shooting-line, and to close the mind to all things except the shooting of the arrow. I have seen George chatting and joking with his target-companions before his turn to shoot, but once on the line this is all forgotten, and it is obvious from the meticulous way he shoots that there is at that moment nothing in his mind but the target, and only the Gold at that.

Next he mentions the need for constant practice, but intelligent thinking practice. The knowledge required to shoot well is gained only by repetition and analysis. With this type of introspective shooting the archer gradually becomes aware of how the various parts of his body contribute to the success or failure of the shot. I might add here that I have heard it said that it is easy to shoot well and difficult to shoot badly. This means that when an archer has such insight to his style that he can duplicate each shot almost effortlessly he will attain excellent scores, but when he loses this awareness of the smooth functioning of every part of his style he will find himself working very hard on his shooting and still finish with a poor score.

George's last point is a little surprising in that he leaves the discussions on will-power and concentration behind and simply says that absolute pin-point attention must be paid to tackle. This brings things down to earth with a bump, but if you think about it it is quite sensible advice, for where will the most perfect style and utmost concentration get you if your serving is slowly coming undone or your arrows are not perfectly straight?

5. Correct grip on the bow

6. Sideview of the correct grip. The proper length of arrow is now in use

7. Incorrect grip on bow

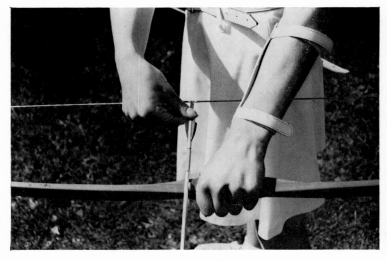

8. Nocking an arrow. Four-fletch in use

9. Before drawing, get arm in a straight line keeping the hand flat

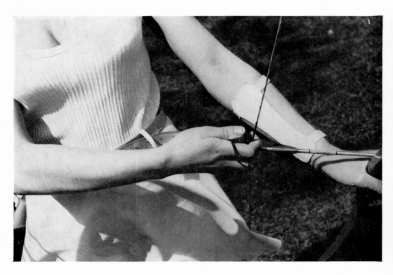

10. *Aids to good shooting*

The last five chapters have shown you how your scores can be increased by diligent practice and attention to every detail of your style, ironing out faults whenever you find them. In addition to the skill which is gradually acquired by your mind and body there are certain refinements to your equipment which will give you additional accuracy, so I now propose to discuss these.

In Chapter 3 we discussed the fitting of a nocking-point on the string, and without a doubt this is essential. Archers who try to make do without one will always find difficulty in getting their vertical alignment correct, because only a small amount of 'pinch' will send the nock a little way along the string, and the archer will never know it. People who cannot be bothered to fit a nocking-point say that they know they are using the same point on the string every time because at that spot the bowstring is cleaner than where the fingers have rubbed, but they can have no idea whether the arrow moves along or not during the draw. The nocking-point binding should be quite small, just big enough to stop the arrow from moving up or down, but no more. Sometimes one sees masses of extra serving either side of the arrow on top of the serving proper, and this is quite unnecessary.

When I told you how to put the nocking-point on the string I said that it should be one eighth of an inch above a right angle, but this is only correct for wooden bows, solid glass-fibre bows, or any bow where the arrow rests on a solid arrow shelf. Almost all composite bows are fitted with an arrow rest made of some flexible material which will give no resistance to the arrow, and with these it is best to put the nocking-point on at exactly right angles.

It is always worthwhile checking that the arrow is at a right angle to the string both before and during a tournament, for sometimes the whole centre serving will slide up the string and this will make your arrow drop lower and lower. Very annoying when you are up with the leaders! This happens to everyone sooner or later, but checking it every time you brace your bow will help you to detect it before it gets too bad. If you find that your serving is slipping change the string immediately, and if you are unprepared and haven't a spare, then start to nock the arrow under the proper nocking-point. Once it starts to go there is little you can do to stop it except to reserve it completely, but when you do a really good job of serving it will resist slipping for a much longer time. When you are stripping the old serving off be very careful not to cut the main string, which can be done very easily if you don't pay attention. Before applying the new serving take the string off the bow and untwist it until there are only a few turns left. Now string the bow again and serve it in the direction of the twist, as tightly as you can. When you have finished you can put the twist back in the string and this will tighten the serving just that little bit more, and it will also help to take up any looseness that may develop with use. When serving it is advisable to start above the nocking-point and work down, and rather than just laying the end of the thread with the strands of the string, pass the end *through* the string before you start. Apply bees-wax to the serving thread as you wind it on for this will hold it in place better and help you to get it tight. Some archers rub a hard setting glue into the serving when they have finished; not very much, just enough to hold the threads together.

The serving should be finished off with some ordinary whipping, which can be tricky if you have never done it before. When you have nearly enough serving, lay a matchstick or knitting needle against the string and serve over this as well, for about half an inch. Now withdraw the matchstick or needle, taking care to hold the extra serving in place so that you finish up with the main string running through a little tunnel of serving. Now pass the end of the thread back through this tunnel and wind the extra serving tightly over it. You will finish up with a loop of spare thread which is pulled through

the serving you have just completed, and then cut off so that
the end is held down under this extra serving. It sounds very
complicated, but if you read this while referring to Fig. 5
you will get the idea.

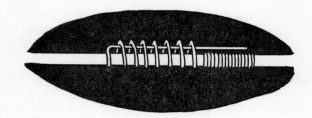

FIG. 5A.

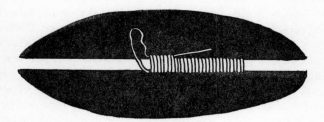

FIG. 5B.

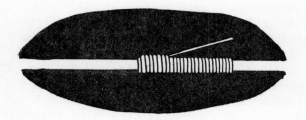

FIG. 5C.

Occasionally one will see an archer with an extra marked
spot on his string about three inches above the nocking-point,
and this is known as a 'kisser', for the simple reason that at

full draw the archer places it between his lips, the idea being that this gives an additional check that the drawing-hand is correctly located under the chin. Unfortunately, I feel that a kisser is of doubtful value for after using one for some time an archer tends to forget that it is only there for a check and begins to rely on it instead of concentrating on getting a firm anchor. As the lips can be pushed far forward of the teeth it is possible for the kisser to be in the correct place even though the string is nowhere near the chin, which is a much firmer place to rely on.

In spite of this criticism, a kisser is a very good idea for archers who have trouble in getting a mark at the longer distance, either through physical incapacity or because the distance between the aiming eye and the chin is unusually short. By using a kisser well up the string the archer can have this between his lips whilst his drawing-hand is somewhere on his chest. This will give him much higher marks on his bow, but is only recommended when there is no other choice. I remember one archer who eventually used this method of anchoring, but not before he had tried another, most peculiar way of getting on target. He could not get a mark at eighty yards, so he shot by anchoring on a two inch thick piece of wood under his chin which he fixed by means of a tape which he tied over his head. It worked quite well, but the sight of the tape tied in a neat little bow on the top of his head drew forth so much ridicule from his fellow archers that he was forced to abandon it, but it shows you to what lengths archers will go to get better scores.

Now let us have a look at arrow-rests. There are a great many varieties available, and all of them are designed to give the minimum resistance to the passage of the arrow. Choice is largely a matter of personal preference, but after you have used it for a few months, check it to see that it is still firm. They are meant to support the arrow firmly, but should not droop or sag as the arrow is drawn back. A member of my evening class, a First class archer, started to get much larger groups than he was accustomed to and we spent considerable time checking on his style to see what he was doing wrong. There was little wrong with his style, the whole trouble was caused by his arrow-rest. As he reached full draw it was bend-ing down under the weight of the arrow and so was ruining his accuracy. He had been using the same rest for five or six years and it was giving up the ghost, so a new one promptly cured the trouble. If only all of one's archery problems could be solved so easily! It would be improper of me to suggest you purchase one make of arrow-rest in preference to any other, but you can easily see what the better archers use, and make sure that when you fix it to your bow that it doesn't roll the arrow away from the side of the bow-window. Don't forget to check it from time to time.

Tournament arrows today are made so alike that not even a Grand Master Bowman could tell the difference between arrows taken from the same set, but it is still worthwhile to number them, and transfers are made for this purpose at a cost of just a few pence. The usefulness of numbered arrows is that they allow you to spot a rogue very quickly. If you are continually having one bad arrow whilst the rest are in a good group, num-bered arrows will immediately tell you if it is the same one each time. If it isn't then it's you, if it is, then the arrow is at fault, probably because you have bent it without realizing it.

While we are talking about arrows we might as well go into the matching of arrows to a bow, and this brings up the sub-ject of 'spine' again. When an arrow is loosed it does not travel forward absolutely straight, but it bends in the middle. This is caused by the inertia of the pile, which resists the forward movement. In effect, the nock moves forward before the pile, and this can only happen by the arrow bending in the middle. Because it is made of a springy material, whether wood or metal, it will not stay bent, but will flex from side to side. This vibration will carry on all the way to the target. Some excellent slow-motion films have been made of this which are available for club showing (see page 149), and it is amazing how much an arrow bends when it is loosed. It looks almost like a fast-moving snake. Now an arrow with a stiff spine will bend less than a whippy one, so its speed of vibration will be different. When an arrow that is perfectly matched to the bow is loosed, it doesn't touch the bow in its passage past at all. The way this comes about is this: as the arrow starts to travel forward so it bends out from the bow and the centre section passes without touching. Then its natural vibration starts to reverse the action. The arrow is travelling forward at the same time, so that as the nock end approaches the bow this in turn moves out and does not touch the bow. Most of the matching of the arrows to the bow is done by the manufacturers who state on the box what weight and type of bow the arrows are meant for, but the archer can get an even more accurate match by 'tuning' his bow. Every bow has a maximum and minimum bracing height, and by varying this within the given limits he can find by experimental shooting which bracing height is best. Of course, he cannot *see* how the arrows bend, they go far too quickly for that, but he can tell by the sound they make and also by the marks they make on the side of the arrow-rest. An arrow which is well matched will leave the bow with a sharp humming sound; a badly matched one will clang as it strikes some part of the arrow-rest or bow. Similarly, the less marking the arrows make on the side of the arrow-rest the better matched they are. This is fairly advanced stuff for it pre-supposes that the archer is loosing exactly the same each time; a newcomer will get 'clangs' for much of the time. I have seen sets of arrows that have become completely flat on some pro-portion of their length, usually just in front of the fletchings, and this has been caused entirely by them hitting the bow during the loose. It is possible that as little as a quarter of an inch difference in the bracing height would have overcome this.

It comes as a surprise to beginners when they first clap eyes on a set of arrows that have been fletched with plastic instead of feathers. The main advantage of these is that they are not affected by wet weather; feather fletchings get very bedraggled when they are shot during rain, and this reduces accuracy because they no longer steer the arrows properly. Plastic fletchings have less air resistance than feathers, so they give better marks at long distances, but they can only be used on bows that have a cutaway bow-window and a fitted arrow-rest; on a beginner's bow where the arrow rests on a hard shelf, plastic fletchings will smash.

Just as there are a great many different types of arrow-rests, so there is plenty of choice when it comes to bowsights. These can be purchased from just a few shillings up to one that costs as much as a cheap composite bow, and here again choice is largely a matter of personal preference. Accuracy lies in the archer, so an expensive bowsight will not make you more skilful than will a cheap one, it will simply make it easier for you to adjust your aim by small amounts. A Master Bowman would still get Master Bowman scores if you exchanged his modern and intricate sight for an ordinary black-headed pin, but he would be annoyed at the difficulty in moving it up a thirty-second of an inch, and he would be perpetually worried in case the pin were to be accidentally knocked out of position. When you are choosing a bowsight your choice will be dictated to some extent by your purse, but in your early days a very simple one will be good enough. Look for one that is easily adjusted but will stay where you put it, and it is also a help if it is fairly easy to mark its position permanently for the different ranges. Make sure that it is of a type that can be fitted to your bow, for some of them are meant to glue on whilst others have provision for screws. Screws should not be put into self-wood bows or solid glass-fibre bows, and if you intend screwing a bowsight to a composite bow make sure that the screws will go into the handle-riser and not into any part of the top limb that flexes on the draw, no matter how little. A bowyer will not honour his guarantee if your bow has broken just where you have drilled a hole for your bowsight. Do you blame him? When you are fitting your new bowsight make sure that it is exactly parallel to the edge of the bow-window. If you put it on just a little crooked you will have to move it in or out as well as up when you change distances.

You will realize by now that it is most important for the arrow to be drawn back the same amount every time, and the better archer you are the more accurately you can judge it, but a beginner is well advised to fit a draw check to the handle of his bow. This is a simple device which any archer can fit in a few minutes, for it is simply a short piece of rubber so placed that the end of it will be in front of the arrow at full draw. Cut up a quarter of an inch wide elastic band and either glue this to the front of the handle so that it sticks up in front of the arrow, or glue it to the front of the bow-window so that it protrudes sideways in front of the arrow. The elastic must be fairly weak so that there is no tendency for it to move the arrow, for this would ruin your accuracy; it should be just strong enough to pop up when the pile has gone past. The advantage of this draw-check is that it really does two jobs: it tells the archer that he has reached full draw by popping up, and it tells him when he is beginning to creep by suddenly disappearing from view as the pile begins to move forward, in other words, it gives a continuous check on draw-length. Nothing in this world is perfect, and the disadvantage of it is that the archer who is very busy trying to get his sight exactly on the centre of the Gold has also got to give a little of his attention to making sure that his draw-check is still upright. However, as beginners have been known to creep by three or four inches I feel that it is the lesser of two evils. If our poor confused, theoretical beginner has arrows that are really too long for him he must give up the idea of a draw-check until he has replaced his arrows with some shorter ones.

An easily-fitted accessory which will serve as a draw-check is the 'clicker'. This is usually a long thin piece of specially shaped spring steel which is fastened to the inside of the bow-window. When the archer puts his arrow on the rest he also places it between the clicker and the bow, so that the clicker is held away from the bow. As he reaches the end of his draw the pile of the arrow slides out from under the clicker which then slaps the side of the bow with an audible 'click', hence the name. It can only click once on each arrow, so if the archer continues to aim after the click he has no way of telling if he is starting to creep.

The clicker was originally introduced to ensure that the archer uses a backwards loose, and to help those with target shyness. The archer comes almost to full draw without disturbing the clicker, and then takes aim. When he is satisfied with his aim he slowly increases his draw, keeping his sight firmly on the Gold. As soon as he hears the click he looses, and thus ensures a backwards loose. It works wonders for people with target shyness, for they are already troubled with involuntary loosing, and they simply tie up their involuntary loose with the sound of the clicker. They know they must not loose until they hear the clicker, so they are able to aim at the Gold without loosing, start their final draw, and loose when they hear the click.

The positioning of the clicker should be done most carefully, for this is going to determine your draw length. Before fitting the clicker, get a friend to stand beside you while you shoot. He can watch you carefully over a series of arrows and tell you where the pile of your arrow is when you are comfortably at full draw. The clicker should be positioned so that it will be operated just as you reach full draw. If it is placed too far forward it will either click too soon or encourage you to shoot in a hunched style, and if it is placed too far back it will distort your style by forcing you to draw beyond your proper draw length. Now and again you will see an archer standing motionless at full draw, looking as though he is aiming extremely accurately, but then you notice that he is going red in the face and the muscles of his neck are beginning to stand up, and then you realize that his clicker is placed too far back and that he is expending all that effort just to get that all important click before loosing.

When you use a clicker you must be sure that it operates before you loose, otherwise if the clicker is still over the arrow it will tear the fletchings off as the arrow goes past.

You will see that most of the top archers use some form of strap which goes around their wrist and the bow, and this is because they prefer an open grip. See PLATES 10 and 11 again. When you first start to shoot you will probably grip the bow with all four fingers, but as you progress you will find that your scores improve if you hold the bow with the forefinger whilst leaving the other three open. Eventually you may find it even better to shoot with a completely open hand, but then the bow will drop to the ground when it is shot unless you strap it to your wrist to prevent it falling. It is quite wrong to have an open hand without a strap, for to do this you will have to grab the bow as you loose, and this will ruin your accuracy. There are several different designs in wrist-straps, but pick one that holds the bow closely to your hand and is comfortable enough for you to forget all about when in use.

While we are talking about leather straps, I might as well mention the chest guard which you will see some archers wearing. I mentioned earlier that the slightest touch of the string against clothing is enough to ruin the accuracy of your shooting, and this is not always caused by loose clothing on the arm. Many archers are unaware that their poor scores are caused by the string catching on the chest or shoulder, for it is not something that can be easily detected. When the archer does find that this is happening, he can help to cure it by deliberately dropping the shoulder and wearing a chest guard of strong leather which will flatten bulky clothing and help to keep it out of the way of the string.

The latest device for helping archers to achieve higher scores is the range of torque stabilizers. They certainly bring benefits to the better archers, but I do feel that they are a waste of money to anyone under First Class. They consist of weights attached to the part of the bow facing the target, and they are usually fixed some way out from the bow by means of strong rods or tubes. They come in two varieties, short ones which are fixed above and below the handle, or one very long one, colloquially known as a 'poker' which is placed just below the grip of the bow. The intention behind the use of stabilizers is to reduce the tendency of bows to swing round on their axis when they are loosed. As well as bows with stabilizers fitted, it is possible to obtain bows with lead or mercury fitted into the handle which inhibits the tendency of some archers to throw their bow-arm when loosing.

The final piece of equipment which will help your accuracy is the very humble footmarker. You know that before beginning to shoot you should always get your feet comfortably apart and so placed that a line drawn through the toes will reach the target, but instead of finding the right position before every end, why not find it just once at the beginning of the shoot and mark it? It is possible to buy footmarkers made especially for the job, but almost any small item will do: two golf tees, two bottle tops, two meat skewers; anything that can be placed on the ground to show where your toes go but small enough not to interfere with anyone else. If you connect them both together with a short length of chain or stout cord you will be able to have your feet at a constant distance apart, and this will also make your footmarkers easier to find when you walk up to the shooting line. Try to avoid using anything that will not be instantly recognizable as somebody's footmarkers, so don't use coins which anyone will pick up instinctively. I knew one archer who for a short while used as footmarkers little plastic models of Robin Hood. Throughout the day other archers carried them triumphantly down towards the targets, holding them up and shouting, 'Hey, look what I've found!'

11. Caring for your equipment

Although the equipment for your early days in archery is not going to cost you a great deal, your later composite bow and tournament arrows are likely to involve you in considerable expense, so you will be well advised to learn how to look after them right from the beginning. The easiest part of caring for your equipment is of course to keep it clean, metal polish for the arrows and furniture polish for the bows. Earth left on arrows will cause them to corrode, and this can be dangerous because if it gets too bad they are liable to break when they are loosed. A corroded arrow will usually break when it is being straightened, so if you lose an arrow in the grass try to find it the same day, because a few days later corrosion will have started. It is not generally realized that the marking ink used to write one's name on clothing will eat into aluminium, and archers who use it to mark their arrows with their name are likely to find later that they have ruined them.

Arrows will rarely become bent through hitting the target unless they hit nails that have been used to secure faces and which have been left in the boss. When they hit legs or stones in the ground they do bend, and it is a skilled job to straighten them. If you want to learn how to straighten arrows don't start with your best set. Use an old one that is of no further use, put bends in it and then try to straighten it. If you haven't got a straightness tester with a dial gauge, a good test for straightness is to support the arrow at its centre of gravity on the thumb and middle fingernails of the left hand while spinning the nock with the thumb and finger of the right hand. If the arrow makes a smooth hissing noise it is straight, but if it rattles it has a bend in it somewhere. This is quite an accurate test, but it takes time to learn how to spin it properly. This only works with an arrow that has all its fletchings;

if there is one or more missing the arrow will rattle whether it is bent or straight.

The piles of arrows can become blunted with time, but it is only a few minutes work to sharpen them up with a file, and this will help to cut down on bouncers. It is the feather fletchings which wear out the quickest, so take care when you retrieve arrows. If they are in the grass instead of the target make sure that the fletchings are clear of the grass before removing them, and then don't lift the arrow, which will bend, but pull it out backwards in the direction from which it came. If the fletchings are completely hidden under grass roots go forward and uncover the pile, and then draw the arrow forwards and out, which will avoid damage to the fletchings. Similarly, when an arrow has entered so far into a target that the fletchings are embedded in the straw, don't try to pull it out but go behind the target and pull the arrow straight through. This sounds drastic, but it does reduce damage to the fletchings. I hope you realize that all this advice applies to fletchings made from feathers, not plastic, which are rigid and which will be damaged whichever way you get them out of a boss.

When your feather fletchings have had a lot of use and are beginning to look bedraggled, hold them in the steam of a boiling kettle and you will be surprised how much they perk up. While we are talking about fletchings, I may as well bring it to your notice that when you want a new set of arrows it is cheaper to buy a set of unfletched arrows and the fletchings than a new set of finished arrows. It is not a difficult job to fletch arrows, provided that you use a proper jig. Where most people go wrong is to think it necessary to put glue on the shaft and the feather separately and let it dry before adding more glue between them to stick one to the other. With this method you certainly get the fletchings on the arrow, but there is usually far too much glue between them.

Try this method instead. Clean the end of the shaft that is to be fletched, with thinners, white spirit or turpentine, and dry it on a clean cloth. Now roughen the surface gently with some fine emery cloth, taking care not to let your fingers, which may be slightly greasy or dirty, touch the prepared surface. Now wipe off the aluminium dust from the arrow. Place the fletching in the jig according to the instructions which came with the jig, and lay a thin bead of glue along the fletching. This is quite difficult, for most people finish up with a series of blobs of glue, but what is wanted is a line of glue which is dead even with no lumps at all. The way to achieve this is to hold the tube of glue between the thumb and forefinger, and rest the little finger on the side of the fletching to give you a good guide. Now run the hand down the fletching, squeezing the glue out as you go. If you have to stop your hand, stop squeezing the glue, and you will finish up with a smooth bead of glue. If it is not right, wipe the glue off and practise getting this bead several times. When I used to make arrows for a living I was told to use one make of glue, and I can honestly say that I have tried many others but none of them come up to the strength of the one I used then, Durofix, made by the Rawlplug Company. Some archers never have satisfactory results, their fletchings are always falling off, and the reason is usually that they have either not roughened the surface of their shaft with emery cloth or they have handled the fletching area with their fingers after roughening. If you really try to keep your fingers off the prepared surface you will get perfect results every time. One last point that I should mention. A feather is a delicate thing very susceptible to pressure. When you have got the fletching in the clamp with just the quill showing, take the pressure off the clamp blades without opening them so that the fletching can adjust itself, for if you glue the feather on without doing this it may well curl some time after you remove the clamp and give you a deformed fletching.

Let us leave fletching now, and continue with the care of arrows. When a shaft hits the leg of a stand it can sometimes be very difficult to get out again, and it is important to pull it from as near the pile as possible. With most metal arrows the pile is not glued in but is a force-fit, and if you pull from the middle of the shaft you may either bend the arrow or separate the pile from the shaft so that you then have the worse job of getting the pile out of the leg. When the pile is a force fit it is not difficult to get it back in place again. Push the pile in as far as it will go, hold the arrow firmly, and hit the pile into the shaft with a block of soft wood until there is no gap between the pile shoulder and the shaft. If you look at your arrows after a few months' shooting you may find a gap appearing on some of them, so use the same method to push the piles in. It may be necessary to clean out earth from the gaps before they will go back properly. Use a wide piece of wood to avoid hitting your own thumb; you won't need telling about this twice.

Now let us have a look at bows. Although modern composite bows can look thin and delicate they are very strongly constructed and stand up to a lot of abuse, but care should be taken not to twist them, which can occur during bracing. At one time steel bows were very popular, and the method used to brace them consisted of putting the lower recurve in front of the left ankle, lifting the bow so that the handle was behind the right thigh, and then pushing the top recurve forward with the right hand until the bow was bent enough to slip the top loop into the nock. This was fine for tubular steel bows, but the wider flat limbs of composite bows can easily be twisted by this method, so please use the way described in Chapter 3. When bracing the bow by the recommended method the bottom nock is under the instep of the left foot, but it should not go under by more than a couple of inches, otherwise as the bow is braced the end of the limb will be forced against the ground. Also shooting a bow with the string not seated in both sides of the nocks will rapidly twist it, so always check this after bracing.

The string should be rubbed with bees-wax regularly, particularly if it is made of linen, which is stronger when it is slightly moist, and the bees-wax will help to keep some moisture in. Even Dacron and Fortisan strings are better for some bees-wax now and then, for it keeps them smooth and free from fluff, which is important for your aiming. If you notice that the centre serving has taken on a lumpy, rippled, look, change it for a new one, for it means that a strand has broken underneath the serving. It is a false economy to wait for another strand to go, for the whole string may break without further warning when you are shooting, and this will shorten the life of the bow.

When the serving on the string becomes worn and you have to replace it, turn the string upside down before re-serving, then your nocking point will come on a different part of the string, which will lengthen its life.

Composite bows should be stored off the ground by means of a rack which will hold them horizontally rather than standing them against a wall, and of course they should be unstrung when not in use. It takes years for a composite bow to lose cast, but a wooden bow will soon follow the string if it is left braced for any length of time. If you are shooting indoors where it is not possible for you to use a ground quiver avoid leaning your bow against the wall while you walk to the targets, for it will eventually get knocked down and this will spoil the polished surface and perhaps damage your bowsight.

Looking after the targets is really a job for the whole club, so all the members should be acquainted with the few simple rules which help you to get a much longer life out of this expensive but essential item of equipment. The most important of all is never to roll them on to the field, which soon breaks down the outer layer. Carry them on your back, or better still, make a trolley for them. When you do carry them, keep your arms close to your sides with the target just resting on your hands. When your arms are spread out it is much harder work and the target will start to bend over your back, which is nearly as bad for it as rolling. To avoid bending during storage, pack them horizontally on shelves, or vertically in slots, but never leaning at an angle against each other.

For many years I firmly believed along with most other archers that when a target is getting old and soft it is a good idea to pour water over it so that the straw would swell and the cords binding it would shrink and tighten up. However, I have been told quite positively by Maurice Egerton, who makes almost all of the targets used in this country, that this is incorrect. He agrees that water makes the straw swell, but says that this makes the string stretch, so that as the straw dries out it remains much more loose in the expanded string. All of his targets are now made with nylon stitching, but even this ean lose its elasticity if the straw is soaked with water to expand it. He says that this treatment would harden a nylon-bound target initially, but it would soon become worse than it was before. So there you are. A small amount of rain will not harm targets, especially if they have got good stout faces on them, for this will dry out naturally. Once they get thoroughly soaked it is a different matter. Try to spread them out and keep them off the ground until they are dry before you put them back into store, and if you haven't time for that put them away but ensure that they are separated from each other so that air can circulate between them to dry them out. If you store wet bosses close together so that no air can circulate they will soon grow large quantities of fungi, and then you might as well throw them away.

A little care during scoring also helps. When you take your arrows out of the target place one hand on the face with a finger on either side of the arrow, then with the other hand grasp the arrow as near to the pile as possible and pull it straight out without twisting. When you place one hand on the target face you ensure that you will not pull the boss forward off the stand, and you will also avoid pulling the face off the boss. This is a good place to mention that you must be sure that nobody is standing behind your arrows as you withdraw, or you may accidentally strike them in the face or chest with the nock of the arrow.

Sometimes an arrow is so firmly embedded in the target that your hand cannot hold it tightly enough to withdraw it, but just slides along the shaft. In a case like this it works wonders if you place your hand over your mouth and blow hard between the fingers. The warmth and the slight deposit of moisture which your breath will give to your hand will normally be just enough to give you a sufficient grip on the arrow to withdraw it.

It doesn't need much of a breeze to blow a target forward on to the ground, so no matter how calm the day, always tie a strong cord to the top of the stand and fasten it to a stake driven into the ground a few yards behind the target. Having done this, remember to tie the top of the boss to the stand, which is every bit as important. I once forgot to do this and had five arrows smashed. It feels awful, so don't let it happen to you.

The stands themselves will gradually get shot away, both by arrows that hit the lower legs and others that penetrate through the back of the boss, so don't keep them in service for too long. Pay particular attention to the place where all three legs are connected together with a bolt, for a weakness here is not quickly noticed but can still result in a collapsed stand and smashed arrows. We all know that the laws of coincidence are very strange, but on three different occasions I have been at tournaments where a friend of mine from Nonsuch Bowmen, Mavis Quinault, has shot an arrow into the leg of a stand with a light bow and the target has immediately toppled over. I try to avoid being placed on her target!

12. *The rules of shooting*

In every sport there must be rules governing the contestants so that everyone starts on an equal footing and the winner is the person who exhibits the most skill. When new rules are introduced by the governing body of the sport to take account of new developments, one can see that the people who drew up the rules have been concerned not only to decide what is fair for all, but have been determined to see that the sport remains archery. For instance, the laws governing bowsights say that anything can be used provided that it does not incorporate lenses or prisms, otherwise you can see that the prizes would go to the archer who could afford to strap on to his bow the best and biggest telescope. Similarly, a few years ago someone in America invented a ring to go on the fingers that held the string and gave the fastest and smoothest loose that I personally have ever managed, but this was banned by the ruling body, and rightly so, because it took away an element of skill from loosing. Students of philosophy may be interested to know that I purchased mine at what I considered to be an exorbitant price exactly one week before I heard the news that they had been banned. If the rules of archery were not so carefully drawn up I am sure that by now some archers would be using rocket-powered arrows guided by radar, and then the prizes would go, not to the best archer, but to the best guidance system.

I feel that the rules governing any sport fall into two main types: those that are in constant use and are known and accepted by everyone, and those that are there to settle disputes and resolve really complicated and subtle points of argument. The full Rules of Shooting, published by the Grand Archery Society, cover every single aspect of shooting in the fullest detail, but a beginner could not pick out what he needs to know from the mass of technicalities. I will describe the rules which are in constant use, and if you can simply learn these few it will be a great help to you when you first visit your club. The more intricate rules can be learned later on, in fact you will no doubt pick them up almost unconsciously as your shooting career progresses. If you never learn the full rules at all it need not matter a great deal, for at every tournament there is a Judge in charge of things who will know absolutely everything about the Rules of Shooting.

The most important part of the rules is that section concerning safety. Because the bow is no longer used as a weapon the public seem to be under the impression that it is no longer dangerous. It is true that the average modern archer uses a bow much lighter in pull than his counterpart in mediaeval days, but the modern composite bow is so much more efficient than the old longbow that it is every bit as lethal. Because of this great care is taken over the safety aspects of archery, and a Field Captain is placed in charge of the shooting to see that it takes place when it is safe to do so. No archer ever shoots before the Field Captain has blown the whistle, because this means that he has checked that everyone is back from the targets and the field is completely clear. When all the archers have shot he will check that everyone really has finished, and he will then blow again to let all the archers know that it is safe to walk to the targets to take the score and retrieve the arrows. One soon gets into the habit of waiting for the sound of the whistle so that it is in no way irksome, but part of one's shooting. If for any reason you wish to draw your bow before the start of shooting, you must do this only on the shooting-line and in the direction of the targets. Even if you have not got an arrow in the bow, you must never draw up when you are off the line.

If you are ever shooting and you hear someone shout out the word 'Fast!' it simply means that you must stop shooting straight away. Even if you can see what the trouble is and it is at the other end of the shooting-line to where you are, it makes no difference, you must stop shooting. Similarly, if you yourself see something which could be dangerous, call 'Fast' to stop everyone from shooting and then indicate to the Field

Captain what the trouble is.

Because these few simple rules are in use every time archers meet, whether it is an important championship or just a few enjoying some casual club practice, accidents never happen in archery, so even if you just shoot in your own back garden with one or two friends, please keep to these rules.

I mentioned earlier that archers shoot six arrows at a time, but they divide these into two groups of three. If there are four archers shooting at one target two of them will shoot their first three arrows, then they will leave the shooting line and the second pair of archers will go up to shoot their first three arrows. When they have shot, the first pair will return to the line to shoot their last three arrows, and finally the second pair of archers will shoot their last group of three. It sounds very complicated, but it is simple in practice, and helps to ensure that all the archers get the same chances of wind and calm spells. Each six arrows shot is called an 'end', so two ends make a 'dozen'. At the beginning of most tournaments the archers are allowed an end which is not scored and which does not form part of the competition. These arrows are called 'sighters' and are for the purpose of judging the weather conditions and making final adjustments to the sight. It is surprising how many archers get good sighters and then cannot do a thing after scoring starts.

When all have finished shooting and the whistle goes, you walk to the target to take your score, but do be careful to avoid any arrows that have fallen short and have come to rest in the grass. They can be difficult to see and the nock can cause a nasty wound in the ankle if you accidentally walk into one. I may as well point out here that if you break an arrow belonging to someone else by carelessness such as walking on it when it has fallen short, then you are expected to pay for it straight away, but if you shoot a companion's arrow when it is in the target, you do not have to pay for it because it could not be helped. If any of your arrows have fallen short you may pick them up on the way to the target, but you should not go behind the target until all the scores have been taken, for it wastes so much of the scorer's time if he is calling someone's name to take his score and that person has wandered off behind the target looking for arrows. So wait for your score to be taken before you go looking for arrows, even if you have only to say 'No score'.

Scoring is done by pointing to the nocks of the arrows whilst calling out their values. The third archer on the target is usually the Target Captain with the job of taking the scores, and the fourth archer is the Target Lieutenant with the job of checking that they are correctly called. The modern British target is four foot in diameter, and it has five rings on it. The dead centre is called the 'pinhole' and it should be exactly 130 cm. above the target line. The target should slope at an angle of 15 degrees which means that for the pinhole to be immediately above the line the front legs of the stand will have to be a little forward of the line. The centre circle which contains the pinhole is called the 'Gold' because of its colour, never the bull's-eye, and it scores nine points. The next ring is the Red, which scores seven, then comes the Blue which scores five. After this comes the Black at three points, and finally the White, which scores one. Around this is a further narrow band of black to give a clearly defined boundary to the White, but it is important to remember that this is completely within the white scoring area, so a hit on this black edging line scores one. The values are easy to remember if you keep in mind that it is all the odd numbers from one to nine. On International faces there are the same colours, but each colour is further divided into two equal-width zones, so there are ten zones altogether, and these are numbered from one to ten. Try to remember the British scoring first so that you know what each band of colour is, then it is comparatively easy when using a ten-zone face to add on a bonus point when you have hit the inner ring of a colour. This is quicker than laboriously counting in from the edge of the target until you come to each arrow.

When an arrow has struck the dividing line between two colours it counts the higher score, except in fairgrounds. It has only just got to cut the line, so if there is any doubt call over the Judge or Field Captain to give a decision. Where there is doubt over whether the arrow has cut the line or not, do not touch the target face or the arrow until the decision

has been given, for it is a rule that when either of these has
been touched the score given to the arrow must be the lower.
Now and again an archer will do the 'Robin Hood Trick', in
other words he will split another archer's arrow down the
middle. If the second arrow stays embedded in the first then
it takes the score of the first arrow, but if it is deflected into
the target then it is scored according to where it landed. When
an arrow is seen to bounce from the target the archer should
wait until everyone has finished shooting, then he should stand
on the shooting-line with his bow held in the air, the recog-
nized signal for a 'bouncer'. The Field Captain will come
along to check that the arrow is lying on top of the grass in
front of the target, showing that it was indeed a bouncer, and
will then inspect the arrows in the target to see if any of the
nocks have been damaged. If one of them is, then the arrow that
bounced will be given the same score as the struck arrow, but
if no damage can be seen then it will be assumed that the
arrow bounced from the target face and the Field Captain will
allow the archer another shot.

When you are asked to give your score, point to your arrows
as you call, start at the best one, and work down to the lowest.
It is customary to call them three at a time, because this
avoids confusion when there are several arrows with the same
score, for example: nine, seven, seven, pause; seven, seven,
five. It is quite wrong for you to write your score in your own
notebook and then to call it out from this. Many archers do
try to call their score in this manner, but a good Target Captain will soon put them right, for although there is no intention of cheating on the part of the archer concerned it is bad
manners to the other archers on the target who are calling
their scores properly.

When all the arrows have been scored the arrows can be
withdrawn, and it is usual when both sexes are shooting together for the ladies to take theirs first. Sometimes one archer
will take out all the arrows and then sort them out to their
right owners, but this should not be done unless he has asked
permission first. It can be annoying to want to have a look
at what sort of group you have got only to find that a target-
mate has taken out your arrows along with his. When the

arrows have been withdrawn no archer can complain that his score has been taken down incorrectly. If it is at variance with his own score pad then the score on the official board must stand. All the while the arrows are in the target the score can be queried, but not afterwards.

Towards the end of the year when the targets have had a lot of use it often happens that an arrow will penetrate so far that not only can the fletchings not be seen, but even the nock is not visible, although the shaft is still sticking out of the back of the boss. In cases like this the Target Captain will withdraw the arrow and re-insert it in the back of the boss at the same place and at the same angle until the pile comes through the face so that it can be scored. If the boss is so soft that arrows go straight through and into the ground they are not scored, so complain to the Judge or Field Captain and get a replacement.

Sometimes an archer will mis-nock so that when he looses there is a clatter and the arrow drops to the ground a little way ahead of the shooting-line. If the archer can touch the arrow with his bow without moving his feet from either side of the line, then it does not count as being shot and he can shoot another in its place. If he hasn't got another arrow he must get the Judge's permission before going forward to pick it up. Many archers are under the impression that they must pull the arrow back over the line by hooking it with their bow, but this is not so. The rule says that they must be able to *touch* it with their bow before retrieving it, but of course making sure that they are in no danger from archers on either side of them.

When you are on the line shooting your three arrows you must not receive any indication on where your arrows are going from anyone. When you return from the shooting-line your friends may tell you the exact position of every arrow, but when you are on the line there must be no murmured numbers, no 'thumbs up' signs, nor anything at all that would give you an indication of where your shafts are striking.

If by mistake you happen to shoot seven arrows instead of six at one end you are penalized by losing the value of your best arrow. It certainly stops you doing it.

Once you have learned these few rules you will be able to shoot at any club or tournament without giving the game away that you are a newcomer, so do try to remember them; it won't take you very long.

At your new club you will hear snatches of conversation like 'I got a 640 York last week, how did you make out in your Long National?' In this rather mysterious conversation the archers concerned are simply talking about different 'Rounds' they have shot. Instead of shooting for a certain length of time or until they have grown tired, archers shoot these Rounds, which are various combinations of arrows shot from different distances. For example, the York Round referred to consists of six dozen arrows shot from 100 yards, four dozen shot from 80 yards, and finally two dozen arrows shot from 60 yards. The figure of 640 the archer referred to was simply his score when all the arrows had been added together. Although the Round consists of 144 shots, I do hope you realize that the archer shoots the same six arrows over and over again. The usefulness of Rounds is that they enable an archer to compare one day's shooting with another's, and he can compare his own shooting standard with another archer's even if the other archer shoots at a different ground and on another day. When my friend 'Tiger' Loch-head shoots a 640 York in New Zealand I know exactly what standard he is reaching and how it compares with my own.

The York Round is the usual Round which men shoot at tournaments, because it is the longest and most difficult, but there are a good many other ones which are not so difficult, and here is a list of most of them.

YORK
6 dozen arrows at 100 yards
4 dozen arrows at 80 yards
2 dozen arrows at 60 yards

WESTERN
4 dozen arrows at 60 yards
4 dozen arrows at 50 yards

ST GEORGE
3 dozen arrows at 100 yards
3 dozen arrows at 80 yards
3 dozen arrows at 60 yards

NATIONAL
4 dozen arrows at 60 yards
2 dozen arrows at 50 yards

NEW WESTERN
4 dozen arrows at 100 yards
4 dozen arrows at 80 yards

NEW NATIONAL
4 dozen arrows at 100 yards
2 dozen arrows at 80 yards

HEREFORD
6 dozen arrows at 80 yards
4 dozen arrows at 60 yards
2 dozen arrows at 50 yards

ALBION
3 dozen arrows at 80 yards
3 dozen arrows at 60 yards
3 dozen arrows at 50 yards

LONG WESTERN
4 dozen arrows at 80 yards
4 dozen arrows at 60 yards

LONG NATIONAL
4 dozen arrows at 80 yards
2 dozen arrows at 60 yards

WINDSOR
3 dozen arrows at 60 yards
3 dozen arrows at 50 yards
3 dozen arrows at 40 yards

AMERICAN
30 arrows at 60 yards
30 arrows at 50 yards
30 arrows at 40 yards

SHORT WINDSOR
3 dozen arrows at 50 yards
3 dozen arrows at 40 yards
3 dozen arrows at 30 yards

ST NICHOLAS
4 dozen arrows at 40 yards
3 dozen arrows at 30 yards

FITA (Gentlemen)
3 dozen arrows at 90 metres
3 dozen arrows at 70 metres
3 dozen arrows at 50 metres
3 dozen arrows at 30 metres

FITA (Ladies)
3 dozen arrows at 70 metres
3 dozen arrows at 60 metres
3 dozen arrows at 50 metres
3 dozen arrows at 30 metres

If you have just started shooting I would recommend the St Nicholas or the Short Windsor, which is probably a little better because it has three distances which will give you more practice in altering your bow-sight. Don't forget that in any Round the longest distance is shot first, so as you go closer to the target your sight must be put up. These two Rounds are really for Juniors under eighteen years of age, so if you are older than this try to move on to the Rounds where the maximum range is 60 yards as soon as you can. Continual shooting at short ranges will soon wear the centre of the targets out.

The list of Rounds looks very complicated and you cannot imagine learning them off by heart, but if you study them closely you will see that many of them have similarities that make them easier to remember. You will see that the St George, the Albion, and the Windsor all have the same number of arrows, they are just shot over different distances, and you will find that many other of the Rounds can be matched up in this way. Don't make a mistake over the American Round. This is the only Round that does not have a complete number of dozens at each distance.

All of these Rounds except the two FITA's use the standard four-foot five-zone British target. In the two FITA Rounds the four-foot ten-zone targets are used at 90, 70, and 60 metres, but at 50 and 30 metres ten-zone faces only 80 centimetres in diameter are substituted. It comes as a bit of a shock to come down from 70 metres to 50 metres, only to find that the target doesn't look any bigger! You will be shooting for some time before you attempt a FITA Round, but when you come to measure out the ground for this the following table taken from the Rules of Shooting will be a help to you.

	Yards	Feet	Inches
30 metres equals	32	2	5.10
50 metres equals	54	2	0.50
60 metres equals	65	1	10.20
70 metres equals	76	1	7.90
90 metres equals	98	1	3.30

13. *Competitions*

Whenever a club secretary arrives with a handful of duplicated sheets of paper and calls 'Who wants some tournament entry forms?' the old hands rush forward but the beginners rarely move. Newcomers to archery always imagine that they have to be shooting really well before they can go to their first tournament, but this is quite incorrect. I am not suggesting that a beginner with a rather tired 28 lb wooden bow should enter for a York, for his bow will never reach 100 yards, but at a good many tournaments a shorter round for beginners will be included, such as a Western or American, and newcomers should most certainly enter for these. Have a look at the entry form to see what the longest distance is, and if your bow will reach it then enter, even if you don't expect to get more than one arrow out of every six on the target.

When most beginners are urged to enter a tournament they usually make some excuse along the lines of 'everyone will laugh at me because I'm so terrible', but I assure you that this is not true. This is not because the top archers are such kind and considerate people; they may be, but the reason nobody will laugh at you is that they will be far too concerned with what they themselves are scoring to worry about your arrows. When an archer asks you how you are doing, just start to tell him and you will notice that his eyes take on a peculiar glazed look as he pretends to listen while he is thinking about his own scores. So send off your entry form and stop worrying about looking a fool.

If I were to be asked the definition of a tournament, I would say that it is a competition open to archers from any club, who on payment of an entry fee shoot a stated Round together, with prizes being given to those who shoot the best scores; but this simple definition would not give you any idea

of the excitement at tournaments. Shooting week after week
at your own club is certainly enjoyable, with the fun of slowly
increasing your scores and getting to know the other members
better, but over a long period of time there is not a sufficient
challenge amongst a small group of people to keep the interest
strong. At tournaments you will meet people from a great
many different clubs from miles around, and at the really
important tournaments the participants will have come from
hundreds of miles away. Some of these people will become
your personal friends, although you will hardly ever see them
except at archery meetings. You will see a great variety of
archery equipment and you will be able to watch some of the
best archers in the country as they fight it out for the top
places.

When you have decided to enter your first tournament, send
off your entry form with the fee without delay. Archery is
getting so popular these days that some tournaments are full
up within a few days of being advertised. One tournament
which is shot every year at Guildford in Surrey has room for
240 archers, but there are still scores of entries returned for
lack of room.

A week or so before the tournament you will be sent a
Target List which shows the names and clubs of all those
taking part, and which targets they are shooting on. If you
are the third name on your target then you will be the
Target Captain, and you will remember from the last chapter
that this means you will be taking the scores, but don't worry,
if you have difficulty your target companions will give you a
hand.

Always arrive in plenty of time at a tournament, for there
is a lot to do. You will probably have to 'sign in' to let the
organizers know that you are there for there is often a waiting
list of archers hoping for a spare place if someone fails to
turn up. You have to find your own target and get your
equipment ready, and there will always be people you know
to have a quick chat with. Most important of all, you must
leave yourself some time in which to relax so that you can
summon up all your concentration and do your very best.
When you arrive with just a few minutes to spare in which

to get your bow strung and your arrows in your quiver you will reach the shooting-line with your mind in such a panic that a good score will be impossible. So get there early, and relax.

You would be well advised to get your equipment out the night before the tournament and check it over. Has the serving slipped, or does the nocking-point need renewing? Is the bowsight in your tackle box, or have you left it in your other jacket pocket? Make sure that everything is not only present, but also correct.

It is a little ironic that I should give you this advice, for I myself am well known for starting to fletch my arrows as soon as I arrive; I just keep forgetting. I don't feel too bad about it when I remember one well-known archer, whose name I will supply only on personal demand, who once forgot his arrows altogether. The same man once completely refletched his arrows the night before an important tournament, only to find when he started to shoot that he had not left enough room between the fletchings and the nock to take his fingers. On yet another occasion he put his expensive composite bow on the roof of his car while he finished packing and forgot all about it. He drove home and the bow was never seen again. You can see what fun archery can be, can't you?

Let's get back to the tournament. A few minutes before the official time of commencement the Field Captain will call you all together and make a few announcements regarding the running of this particular tournament. He may acquaint you with a recent change in the rules, or it may be a simple 'welcome to the shoot and may the best man win' speech. After this he will give you a few minutes to disperse back to your equipment and then he will blow the whistle for 'sighters', and you are away.

Part of the great thrill of tournaments is the atmosphere of determination which you can feel around you. Even the poorest shots present are trying their hardest to do a little better this time, and the atmosphere can be a little unnerving to a newcomer. If you have got butterflies in your stomach don't worry about your score, but concentrate on your style and then the score will look after itself. This feeling of tension is a great spur to doing well, and if you don't feel the importance of the occasion it wouldn't be quite so much fun, would it?

Although the distances at tournaments are measured very carefully, different weather conditions may mean that you will have to alter your bowsight after the first end. Beginners at competitions seem to belong to two groups: those who alter their sights after every arrow, and those who shoot their arrows off the target all day without considering altering their sights. The ideal is of course between these two; never alter your sight for just one arrow but only for a group, but if you are consistently going off target in one direction, then for goodness sake do something about it.

You may have to shoot for several years before you can expect to finish in the first three places, but at any tournament, including your first one, you may be fortunate enough to win a handicap prize. When you have shot five Rounds at your own club, the club Records Officer will take your scores and work out what your handicap is. He can do this by looking up your scores in the GNAS *Book of Handicap Tables,* and then working out what your average is. This is put on your entry form, and an allowance is given to you before the start of the tournament, according to your standard. If you shoot just a little better than normal during the competition you stand a good chance of taking home a trophy. It may be something quite small, but it's the principle of the thing that counts, isn't it? You will be pleasantly surprised just how many prizes are given at most tournaments; as well as the outright winners and the handicap prizes, there will probably be one for the best Gold, and a hidden score prize which will be decided on by some complicated mathematical system understood only by the organizers. A wooden spoon is sometimes given as a humorous award, but not for the lowest score, which would embarrass the unfortunate recipient, but for the worst White at a particular end, which honour could fall to almost anyone. A very old custom at archery tournaments is the Gold Sweep, in which every archer who wishes to participate pays five pence into a kitty. A two-inch circle is pencilled in the centre of each Gold, but faintly, so that it can only be seen when you are taking the score. Throughout the longer distance, every arrow that strikes this circle is noted on the scoresheet, and at the end of the day the kitty is shared out between all the archers that have struck it, with one share for each arrow. If lots of archers have hit it you may only get your fivepence back, but sometimes you can strike lucky and do much better. At one Surrey Championship several years ago, the Gold Sweep was determined by just one dozen arrows instead of throughout the long distance, and my wife Rose was lucky enough to get one in. We thought she would probably get fifty pence or so for it, but at the prize-giving afterwards she found that she had won the lot, over fifteen pounds! Unfortunately, this custom is dying out to a large extent, for now that archery has entered the Olympics no one wants to be barred just for accepting a few shillings from a Gold Sweep. It's a pity really, for it used to be great fun. I have heard archers say with a big smile, 'He got the medal, but I got the money'!

It is worthwhile buying a copy of the Handicap Tables which I mentioned earlier, for they are very useful to you in that they enable you to compare entirely different Rounds. If you have shot a 340 Western at your club, and then at a tournament you shoot a 290 National, the Handicap Tables will tell you that the National is the better score. As your shooting improves and you return higher scores, your handicap will reduce to keep up with your improved standard.

Tournaments vary in their importance, and the most important ones have what is called 'Record Status'. This means that any high scores made there will be eligible for acceptance as new National Records, so if you shoot a score in your club which is better than the existing National record it will not be acceptable, but if you can do it at a competition that has been accorded Record Status then it will. To obtain this status the organizers have to satisfy the ruling body of the sport that their shoot is properly run, that it is regularly well-attended, and that leading archers usually go to it. County Championships and Regional Championships automatically have Record Status, as have the National Championships, but tournaments

10. Philip Remnant with a good anchor. Perhaps the third finger is a little lazy

11. Two archers with different styles. Can you detect the differences and compare them with your own?

12. Removing arrows from a standard face at a field shoot. It is much more difficult to find those that missed!

13. Cliff Evans using his sixty pound bow at long distance with an instinctive or 'gap-shooting' style

run by clubs are usually organized for several years before they qualify.

As well as the Handicap system there is another method of determining the skill of an archer, and that is the Classification scheme, which divides archers into five different standards. The highest standard an archer can reach is that of Grand Master Bowman. This is so high that at the time of writing there are only two such archers, Richard Hemming from Birmingham, and Lynne Thomas who lives near Cardiff. They are the only people currently at this standard out of about 10,500 archers, so you can see how difficult it is. Here are the scores you must reach if you want to join them. Men need Yorks of 1,000 and FITA's (the International Round) of 1150, and Ladies need Herefords of 1,000 and FITA's of 1,000. Two York/Herefords and two FITA's must be shot in one year and they must be at tournaments organized by FITA, GNAS, or a Region. County Championships and shoots run by clubs do not qualify. These scores will not mean much to you until you start shooting the Rounds mentioned, but then you will realize how fantastically high the standards are. To become a Grand Master Bowman you will have to give your shooting absolute devotion and dedication.

Below this almost impossible peak is the next highest standard of Master Bowman, which was the highest until a few years ago. The scores required are 900 for a Ladies' Hereford, 850 for a Men's York, and 1,000 for a Ladies FITA and 1050 for a Men's FITA. Again four Rounds are needed, but they can be any combination of York/Herefords and FITA's so long as at least one of each is shot. Only two Rounds have to be shot at a competition run by FITA, GNAS, a Regional Society, or a County Championship; the other scores can be made at any other competition or club Target day.

After Master Bowman there is First Class, Second Class, and finally Third Class, the lowest. These classifications can be reached by shooting a great variety of Rounds, so the required scores are not given here, but can be found in the GNAS Rules of Shooting. Three scores of the required standard are needed to qualify, and they must all be shot in one year. All of them can be shot in your own club, so there is no need to go to a tournament at all if you are unable to summon up the courage.

When you have bought a copy of the Rules of Shooting you will see from the standards needed for the different classifications that to reach Second Class men must shoot a Round involving 80 yards, ladies 60 yards, while to reach First Class they must shoot a Round which uses 100 yards, and ladies 80 yards.

This classification scheme is probably more useful to archers than the Handicap system, because although it does not give such an accurate idea of an archer's standard because the range of each level is wider, it does give the archer something much more definite to try for. As your skill improves your handicap automatically improves with it, but to classify you have to reach a certain stated score three times. When you have shot two Rounds of the classification you are trying for, you will put a tremendous amount of concentration into achieving the final one you need.

Whether you are merely trying to improve your handicap, or are attempting to reach a certain classification, anything that will help you to shoot better at a tournament is worthwhile. If you have a bad arrow, a bad end, or even a bad dozen, don't give up. Many times I have lost the will to win just because of a few bad arrows, and then found that I have missed a classification or a prize by one or two points. So no matter what happens, keep trying.

At the end of the tournament there will be an interval during which you can relax and have a bite to eat or a drink or two, but during this there will be a great deal of work done by the organizers, who will be busy working out the scores to find out who are the prizewinners. The prize-giving can be a tense time for all those who think that they may be in the running. It really is marvellous when your name is announced for the first time, and you have to walk up to the table for your prize. It is even better when you arrive home and say 'Look what I've won!'

14. *Starting your own club*

Many archery clubs are started by people who already have some experience of archery, and of course, this does give them considerable help because they will know people who can help with coaching or other advice, and they will already have a fair amount of knowledge on how archery is organized.

However, the reader of this book may be a newcomer to the sport, he may not know of any archers who could help him, and he may have already found out that there is no archery club within many miles, so this chapter is for him. But before you start to organize a club, be warned. Starting any club involves work, and so does keeping it running once you have started it, so do make sure that you have enough enthusiasm to see you through before you involve other people's time and energy. Right, let's go.

The more people you can get to join your archery club the healthier, richer, and more enthusiastic it will be. By far the best method of finding your new club members is by writing to the local Press. Perhaps in a few years' time it will be better to get an interview on local radio or television, but at the present time the Press is best. Putting notices in the windows of your local sports shops and public libraries will bring in a few enquiries, but nothing like so many as a letter to the Editor in your local newspaper. Send him a short letter, saying that you are hoping to start an archery club and would anyone interested write to you. Don't allow your letter to become an advertisement for archery by saying how cheap the basic equipment is, how much fun it is, and how we will all get a really good club going. This would be a mistake, for the shorter your letter, the more chance you will have of getting it published. Everyone knows that archery consists of shooting arrows at a target, and the shortest of letters will get you an adequate response from all those people who have always been interested in the sport but have never before done anything about it.

Include your phone number in your letter, for most people hate writing and would much sooner give you a ring, but do keep a pencil and paper handy by the telephone so that you can be sure of getting every caller's name and address. Within a few days of your letter appearing you will have a good idea of how many members your embryo club is likely to have, and you can go ahead with plans for getting them all together at a meeting. If the response is small, don't be disappointed but remember the saying about oaks and little acorns. Six enthusiasts are worth more than two dozen dilettantes. If there are only a few people who contact you, then perhaps the first meeting can be held in your own living-room, but it is more likely that there will be sufficient numbers to warrant the hiring of a public room or hall. With a firm idea of the number of people likely to be present, visit your local town hall or library, or even your local public house, and ask about the use of a room for a meeting. Remember that a smaller room that is crowded will generate more enthusiasm than a large hall with the same number of people in it, for they will get to know each other more quickly and the atmosphere will be more free and easy. Although the hiring charge for this first meeting will probably have to be paid for out of your own pocket you will find that a room can be obtained quite cheaply. At the risk of offending teetotallers, I have always found that public houses are frequently the cheapest and altogether the most helpful, probably because the landlord will have hopes of future customers. He can also give you an answer on availability and hire charge there and then, or at the latest within a day or two, whereas town halls and libraries often have to put the request before a committee which is due to meet in three months' time, by which time all your prospective archers will have taken up bowling or darts.

Having got your meeting place, each person who enquired must be sent a letter stating the date, time, and place of the inaugural meeting. If you have a large number of people to write to then it may be duplicated, but it is most important that it is enthusiastic and friendly. Your letter need not be long, and again there is no need to write a lecture on archery, but it will be worthwhile spending time on it to get the tone just right. The people who receive this letter must feel that archery is going to be very enjoyable, and if they come to your meeting and later on start shooting in this frame of mind then it *will* be enjoyable. This letter is so important because those people who don't come to the meeting will not contact you again; they will be lost for good.

Your new friends will probably know nothing about archery except for the fact that they want to try it, so you must assemble as much information about it as you can for them to discuss. Archery magazines are a very good source of information, with a good many advertisements for you to write to for price-lists, catalogues, etc. Concentrate more on beginner's equipment rather than the expensive composite bows which might well deter your newcomers right at the beginning. I have known people hesitate for weeks before buying the very cheapest beginners' wooden bow, but a few months later when the archery bug has bitten they have cancelled their expensive holiday and given up smoking so that they can buy the latest thing in expensive composites. Write to the ruling body of the sport, the Grand National Archery Society, tell them you are starting a club, and see what help they can give you. Take all this information along with you to the meeting and at least it will look as though *somebody* knows what it is all about!

Whether this first meeting is formal or not depends to a great extent on the number of people present, but as at the beginning few people will know each other it will probably develop better as a general discussion. Eventually a committee must be elected, with a Chairman, Secretary, Treasurer, etc., but it is better at the start to let everyone get to know each other and to discuss the first big problem.

The first big problem and the greatest priority for a new club is to get a shooting-ground. This may seem so obvious as to be not worth saying, but I have heard people discussing how many targets and stands to buy before they have done anything about finding somewhere to shoot, so keep in your mind that the ground comes first. This is a much greater task in towns than in rural areas, but even in the depth of the country it can be difficult to find a field that is suitable. So often a friendly farmer will agree to let one of his fields be used for archery, but then the new archers find that the ground is so rough or overgrown that each end consists of five minutes shooting and ten minutes searching. School playing-fields are always kept in excellent condition and are not much used at weekends, or your local park may have a stretch of open ground that might be roped off for your use.

When you first decided to try to start your own club you probably had a few ideas about where to shoot, but if all your new friends rack their brains I am sure that wherever you live you will finish up with a long list of possible places that might be used by your new club, and some of the members might know the right person to contact to obtain permission. It is much better if you can find the name of someone to write to rather than sending your letter off to someone anonymous like 'The Owner' or 'The Secretary', but do be sure to spell their name correctly. Your letter must be carefully worded and will look better typed rather than hand-written. Remember that if someone lets you use their ground they are doing you a favour, not the other way around, so the tone of the letter must be polite and try to give the impression that you are responsible people, which I hope you are. Mention that you hope to form a club which will have members of all ages so that they realize that you will have older people present who will see that the younger ones don't get up to mischief. People who don't know about archery always assume that a new archery club will mean arrows raining down in all directions, so you might as well mention that all clubs which are affiliated to the GNAS, which yours will be, are automatically insured for £50,000 against accidents.

John Bray, the secretary of the GNAS once had to go to the aid of a new club which had been given permission by the Town Council to use a playing-field, provided that the archers used arrows 'with rubber suckers on the front', so you can see how much the average person knows about the sport.

Your letter should not ask for permission to use the field, it should ask if they would be willing to consider it and to meet you to discuss it, which is a rather different thing. If they write back agreeing to meet you, you are over half-way there, for then you know that they are not averse to the basic idea, but naturally they want to find out more about it and to see what sort of person you are. Before you write to ask about the possible use of a ground check to make sure that it is large enough, otherwise you will appear very ungrateful if you later turn it down because it is too small. The maximum range you will shoot is 100 yards; in addition to this you will need at least ten yards behind the shooting-line and a further thirty or forty yards behind the targets, so you can see that the length of the ground needs to be at least 150 yards long. Don't deceive yourself into thinking that a smaller field will do because you will never want to shoot at 100 yards; one day you will.

Although you need not mention it at this stage, eventually you will also need permission to put up a small garden shed to take your targets and stands.

It may take some time for you to obtain the use of a ground, especially if you are dealing with a local Council, but your perseverance should be successful and then you will need a club committee to get the whole thing under way. This can be elected at the first meeting, or it may be left until later, but you must form your committee by the time you have got the ground. The number of officers on a committee will vary from club to club, but I will discuss the usual arrangement.

Probably the least active member of a Committee will be the President, for he is usually a sort of figurehead. He is often someone who has done a great service to the club, and because of this a club may not have a President at all in its early stages. A good choice would be the person who owns the field you use for shooting, or even a local showbusiness personality. If you don't choose an archer, you want someone who is influential enough to give the club help if it ever runs into trouble.

The Chairman is the most important member on the Committee, for he sets the tone of the meetings, but it is a hard job to do well. Far too many chairmen try to run the club as they want it rather than the way the members want it, so the members must be careful in their choice. A good chairman should impart his enthusiasm to the rest of the club but he should always find their views on things rather than imposing his own. At committee meetings in particular a good chairman will insist that things are run in an orderly manner without everyone talking at the same time, but he must also make sure that the newest person on the committee has his say. He has also got to have the ability to shut up those people who would talk for hours on end, without giving them any offence.

If you are the person that starts the new club you will probably finish up as Secretary, for this is the job needing the most work. The club secretary deals with all the correspondence, which can be quite considerable, keeps the minutes at meetings, answers the hundred and one queries that come from the members, and carries out many of the jobs that the committee decides on. A good secretary is worth his weight in Golds.

When you are thinking of whom to choose for Treasurer it is worthwhile finding out if any of the members deal with accounts in the course of their everyday work. I am not suggesting that they are likely to be more honest than anyone else, but the work will come much more easily to them, and most important of all, they will do the job with much more attention to detail. Most people elected to the position of treasurer would make a reasonable job of it, but someone whose daily work involves accounts will have every item meticulously entered in their books, and will be able to tell the secretary without a moment's hesitation how the club stands for money. As well as keeping a record of the accounts he is usually the one to chase the members for their subscriptions, which can be quite difficult at times.

If you have a member who you know likes getting up early in the mornings, then make him the Field Captain. His job is to be responsible for safety during shooting, in other words, he blows the whistle. In addition to this, in most clubs he sees that the field is correctly measured out before shooting starts, and also that the targets are put out properly. He doesn't actually have to do the work himself, he must just make sure that it gets done. So often the Field Captain gets to the state where he is doing the whole job on his own and then rapidly becomes disenchanted with archery and leaves the club. If he is sensible he will start the right way and refuse to commence work until he has help, and lots of it.

Finally, we come to the Records Officer. He will not have much work to do at the beginning, but it will build up as the club becomes established. His job is to keep a record of all the scores shot by the club members and to establish their handicaps with the aid of the sets of GNAS Tables. It is one of those jobs which need not take more than half an hour every week, but which builds up to a monster job if it is not done regularly. Special loose-leaf books are obtainable for keeping the records, which makes the work much easier. As well as keeping a check on the archers' handicaps he confirms their classifications as they reach each stage. If he is really keen on his job he can make up a board to go on the wall of the club house which will show at a glance each archer's classification and handicap. A board like this certainly encourages everyone to shoot better because if everyone can see the standard of every archer in the club they will all tend to try that little bit harder.

These then are the main officers of the committee, although each club may alter them as their own needs dictate. It is advisable to have in addition to the officers two or three extra members on the committee with no specific tasks, but who can give a wider base for decisions taken.

As soon as the club has been properly formed and the committee elected, they must send off an application to join the Grand National Archery Society. Until your club is affiliated to this body you will not be insured against accidents, and your members will not be able to enter competitions. Until your club joins the GNAS you will be cut off from all the interesting and exciting things going on in the sport, for joining the parent body also makes you a member of your County organization, the Region, and the World authority, Federation Internationale de Tir à l'Arc, know to archers as FITA for short.

The next task before the new committee is the formulation of a club constitution, the rules which control the running of the club. Try to make this readable and easily understood rather than quasi-legal and precise. Experience has shown me that a constitution can never cover every case that will arise, and after all, if the club members are going to argue over the exact meaning of articles in the constitution then your club is in a bad way. When the committee have decided on a Constitution which they feel is suitable for their club they should present it at a meeting of all the members, and go through it clause by clause. This is where you need a firm chairman to keep things going along at speed and keeping everyone on the point being discussed. I am not saying that the members should be forced into accepting the Constitution as presented by the committee, but the chairman must not let the meeting degenerate into a long rambling discussion on points of very little importance.

An important part of the Constitution and one which may provoke argument is the amount of the annual subscription. The biggest expenditures of most clubs are the rent of the shooting-ground and the provision of targets, so your subscriptions must be related to these. The expenses of a new club are heavier in the first year because all the targets have to be bought new, but in subsequent years only a proportion of the targets will have to be replaced. Target stands will also be needed and are quite expensive, but these can easily be made by the club members. Allow one target for each six members, for although they will rarely all come along together on any one occasion, you could accommodate them if they do. Regarding the amount of the subscription, I know some clubs who have a deliberately high subscription rate so that they can build up a big bank balance 'in case of emergencies', but I feel that this policy can be carried too far. Surely it is more sensible to keep the subscriptions low and therefore encourage more people to join, so long as your income does exceed the expenditure by a few pounds. In every club there are members who shoot no more than half a dozen times a year but who are perfectly willing to pay a reasonable subscription, but these people would drop out altogether if the annual fee were too high.

In addition to an annual subscription some clubs have a

shooting fee of a few pence which is payable each day an archer shoots, but I would not recommend it. It gives a lot of work to the secretary or treasurer who has to collect it, and there are always people who have no change or forget to pay up. It is much better to have an annual subscription which covers everything; you can always raise it at the A.G.M. if it is insufficient.

I feel that that is all the help I can offer you on starting your club; the rest will come to you as you go along, but I would like to offer you some advice on how to keep it going. So often one hears of a club that has started on a great wave of enthusiasm and then after two or three years the members dwindle away until there is no club left. This is not just in archery clubs for examples come to mind in almost any sport or hobby, but why does it happen? So often the problem is caused by a clash of personalities within the ranks of the committee. Perhaps the chairman and the secretary disagree on the way things should be run, and so the club members form two groups according to which person they support, and the club is doomed. All the members of the committee should realize that it is the club as a whole that is important, not their own individual likes and dislikes. A good chairman and secretary will build up a strong club spirit so that all disagreements are resolved in a friendly fashion. In committee meetings in particular, a good chairman will keep the temperature down by seeing that matters over which there is disagreement are discussed in a calm manner, with only one person speaking at a time. When all the pertinent points of view have been put a democratic vote is taken, and from then on all the committee should back the decision, including those who were opposed. It is quite wrong for those who were in the minority to keep any issue alive amongst the club members after a decision has been reached.

Sometimes there is no friction at all within the club, but still the membership dwindles, and the usual reason for this is that not enough notice is being taken of newcomers. Every club will gradually lose members, not through dissatisfaction, but for simple reasons like leaving the district, needing more time for study, work to do at home, etc., so every club must replace these losses with newcomers. I am sorry to say this, but so often someone new will visit a club and say that they are interested in taking up archery, then after a few minutes conversation they will be completely ignored while the members go back to their shooting. It need not be the same person every week who gives up his shooting to look after newcomers, but someone should volunteer to put a bow in their hands and start them off with some simple instruction. My own club runs a beginners' course at the beginning of the year which is always well publicized by letters to the Press before it begins, and this helps us by getting most of the newcomers together in one bunch instead of seeing a fresh face for every week in the year. We always lend them discarded equipment free of charge for the first two or three weeks, but after this we insist that they buy their own. It is much easier to teach people who have got their own equipment, and it also means that we lose those who really have no intention of taking up the sport but who will continue shooting all the while it costs them nothing. Using club equipment for the first two or three weeks means that when they do buy their own equipment, they are able to get exactly the right size.

Although I recommend that you lend equipment to beginners for the first few weeks, on no account should you let them take it away from the club. At one time I was happy to lend equipment of my own to beginners, but as a result of this I have lost several tabs and armguards, and even a complete set of Silver Streak arrows which I was never able to recover. All of your beginners may turn out to be fine people who are a credit to your club, but it may be several months before you are sure of this, so keep your equipment safe.

All beginners' courses should be thought out well in advance, and the person running it should know what he intends to teach each week. Twenty yards is a good distance to shoot for the first couple of lessons, but this could be increased by ten yards each lesson until they have reached sixty yards, which brings several different Rounds within reach. For the first few lessons the targets should be set up and the field marked out all ready for the class, but after this the new archers should be encouraged to do this work themselves, and to clear away afterwards. It makes them begin to feel like members of a club instead of temporary guests. When the course is over and your newcomers are able to look after themselves, it is important that they are not left to shoot on their own. Many of your more experienced archers will want to shoot Rounds involving eighty and one hundred yards, but they must be encouraged to shoot American and Western Rounds with the newcomers for a little while so that they all get to know each other. Avoid having the new archers on their own targets but instead mix them up with the old hands, for this is an important stage in their transition to full club members.

When you have gained new members a great help in keeping them is to organize a social side to the club. It does not need to be too elaborate, a simple thing like the secretary finding out how many people would like to visit a theatre where there is a particularly good show on can result in an enjoyable evening, or perhaps one of the members has a living-room large enough for the club to hold a bottle-party. Remember that these occasions must be for the whole club and not just for a particular group who get on well together: you must not leave out particular individuals just because they seem a bit dull. If they have paid their subscription they are as entitled as anyone to attend a club function, and they may well blossom out when they feel accepted.

The purpose of an archery club is to encourage shooting, so social events should not be arranged too often, three or four times a year should be enough. More often than this and some of the members may find that they cannot afford it, and then they will begin to feel left out. It's quite difficult keeping everybody happy, isn't it?

Finally a few words addressed to the club secretaries who will have to do most of the work in getting people to attend all these social events, club target days, club championships, matches against other clubs, committee meetings, annual general meetings, and all the other events that you will have to raise support for. It is this: there is no substitute for actually asking people. If you pin an announcement on the club notice board, with a space for interested people to sign their names, you will be very lucky to get more than four or five signatures, no matter how keen you think your club is. The only way to get people to enter things or give you their help is to ask them yourself, personally. There is no need to twist their arm; few people ever bother to read notices, and the mere fact that you have asked them face to face is usually enough to get an affirmative. In addition, they know that if they don't do it they will have let you down. No coercion is necessary, just ask them nicely, and make sure that you don't miss anyone. All club work is voluntary, so be sure to thank people who help out; it makes them more willing the next time.

15. *Field Archery*

This book is mainly about Target Archery because that is the most popular form of the sport in Britain, and it is very well organized throughout the whole world. But there are other forms of shooting with the bow and arrow which you may want to try one day, and the most important of these is Field Archery. This takes place in woods and rough fields rather than on nicely mowed lawns, and is much closer to the Robin Hood sort of shooting. Interest in Field Archery in this country has grown tremendously over the last few years, and as it has grown it has changed, both in its rules and in the style of shooting. Today there are two quite separate organizations which cater for this form of archery in Britain, The Grand National Archery Society (GNAS), and the English Field Archery Society (EFAA). The GNAS is the long-established body which has controlled Target Archery in this country for over a hundred years and is now also catering for field archers. It is affiliated to FITA, the international ruling body for Target. The EFAA is affiliated to the International Field Archery Association, and is a fairly new organization, but it has plenty of enthusiasm. If you are a new archer wanting to do Field-Shooting, there is no need to ponder over which society to join; become a member of both and then you can go to *all* the available shoots.

Most of the information in this chapter has come from shoots organized by my good friends the Panther Bowhunters of Brentwood, Essex. They are members of the EFAA, so I am writing about EFAA rules, not GNAS, although a field archer would feel quite at home at shoots organized by either body.

In Target Archery the competitors shoot at one target throughout the Round, simply changing to a shorter distance after a set number of arrows, but in Field the archers form into groups of between four to six people who then walk round the course shooting at the targets as they come to them. There are usually twenty-eight targets divided into two courses of fourteen each, but if the available ground is not large enough to accommodate all these, then there will be only fourteen targets altogether and all the archers will go round the course twice.

The distances vary tremendously, for the first target on a course may be only eleven yards away, and then you may find when you walk along to the next target that it is eighty yards away. Not so very long ago the distance from the shooting line to the target was always unknown to the archers, but it is now becoming more and more the practice to mark the distances, so that people who have previously engaged only in Target Archery can go to their first Field Shoot without any worries about where to aim or how to guess distance. They will shoot in their normal style except that they will have to adjust their bowsight for each target.

Because the distances vary so much different diameters of faces are used, four in all: six inches, twelve inches, eighteen inches, and finally twenty-four inches. There are only two scoring zones, an outer circle scoring three, and an inner circle which is half the diameter of the outer, scoring five. Each archer shoots four arrows at each target, so his maximum score possible on each target is twenty. In the centre of each target there is a small additional circle, but this does not give a higher score; it is there simply to give the archers something more definite to aim at.

The types of round shot are determined by the types of faces used, the various distances, and the method of scoring. There have been several different types in the past, but today only two are normally used, the Field Round (sometimes called the Standard Round) and the Hunter Round. On the faces used in the Field Round the outer three-zone is black, the inner five-zone is white, and the aiming spot is black. This is the face in use in Plate 12. The Hunter Round uses faces which are entirely black except for a white aiming spot in the centre. The scoring is again five and three, but the scoring rings are printed in dark grey and are invisible from the shooting position. The archers shoot at the white aiming spot, but cannot see which zone they have struck until they walk up to the target. On some of the faces the scoring zone is much smaller than the total width of the face so the archers can be very disappointed when they have seen their arrows strike but find when they get close that they are all outside the three zone.

Some of the targets are 'walk-ups' which simply means that the archers shoot their four arrows from different positions, each one closer than the one before. Pegs are placed in the ground to mark the shooting position and the archer would normally shoot from behind these pegs. When only one peg is provided the archers shoot all four arrows from this spot which enables them to adjust their aiming after the first arrow, but of course on walk-ups each shot is from a different distance and this is much more difficult.

Because of the difficulty involved in carrying heavy targets over rough country most field courses are laid out permanently. Straw bales are used to put the faces on instead of the circular bosses used in Target, and they are often mounted on wooden platforms a few inches off the ground and fitted with a plastic or canvas cover to stop them rotting. When a club first sets out its course it registers it with the EFAA, who inspect it to see that it conforms with the regulations regarding safety, and then that club is covered by the EFAA, insurance scheme. The club may request that its course be 'Chartered', which means that it conforms with all the regulations so that scores made there will be accepted towards an archer's classification. Someone like Paul Wiskin, who is Regional Range Charter Officer for the Eastern Region of the EFAA will inspect the course and make sure that the distances and sizes of face are correct for all the targets, that there are clear lanes from the shooting positions to the targets, and that generally everything about the course is satisfactory. When a club has a Chartered range it will normally throw it open on one Sunday each month to members from other clubs so that they can try for scores of higher classification. Because the distances and sizes of targets in a Chartered course

are exactly specified, a similar situation to that existing in a
Target Round arises, in that a score made in one part of the
country can be compared directly with one made somewhere
else. I feel sure that this is a major advance in Field and will
do a great deal to popularize the sport.

At the monthly Classification shoot a club would normally
expect about sixty people to shoot, while at an Open Tournament where prizes are given the number would normally be
around 150. When several clubs in a Region arrange their
Classification shoots on different Sundays throughout the
month, all the archers have the choice every weekend of either
shooting on their own ground for practice or travelling to
another club to try to improve their classification. The classification system is very similar to that in Target Archery in
that the archer has to reach certain scores to qualify.

At any Field Shoot the archers will be divided into three
Divisions, according to their style of shooting. The easiest of
these to explain is the one known as 'Freestyle' which means
that the archer is permitted the use of a sight. Everything that
I have written in Chapters 4-10 in this book is also intended
for the freestyler for the two styles are the same, except that
the freestyle Field Archer has got to calibrate his bowsight in
much smaller intervals to allow for the much greater variety
in target distances. If a freestyle Field Archer should go to a
shoot where the distances are *not* marked, he has to estimate
the distance of each target and set his bowsight accordingly.

The second style which is probably still the most popular is
known as 'bare-bow', and here the regulations are more intricate. The most important point here is that the part of the
upper limb above the arrow-rest extending for the length of
the bow-window must be free of markings of any sort. This
doesn't mean only distance marks, it also includes patterns in
the limb material or marks caused by damage. Any marks like
this should be covered with tape. If the archer uses a clicker
in his shooting it must be of a type that is fitted underneath
the arrow, for if it were to be fixed to the side of the bow-
window above the arrow, different parts of it could be used
for sighting. There must be no visible marks on the bowstring,
and the serving must be of one colour. Finally, the archer may

use only one nocking point and one arrow-rest. These rules
ensure that archers in this class are not using any form of
sight.

Bare-bow archers use an entirely different method of aiming
which is based on the position of the arrow pile in relation
to the target, and this is known as 'gap-shooting'. Almost without exception, bare-bow archers anchor at the side of the face
with the middle finger of the drawing hand at the corner of
the mouth, as in PLATE 13. With this anchor, most archers
will find that when they get the pile of their arrow on the
centre of the target at a distance of about sixty yards, the
trajectory of their arrow will be such that it will fall into the
centre of the target. This distance will vary from one archer
to another because of differences in weights of bows, personal
techniques, etc., but sixty yards is about average for a man.
Now when he goes back to seventy yards he will have to raise
the angle of his arrow so that now the pile will be on the top
of the target, and at eighty yards the pile may be over the top
of the target altogether.

At ranges below sixty yards the archer will need to flatten
the angle of the arrow, so at fifty the pile may be on the
bottom of the target and at ranges below this the pile will be
lined up underneath the target. At these shorter ranges the
archer sees a vertical gap between the pile of the arrow and
the centre of the target, and it is this gap which the archer has
to estimate. Gap-shooters are less dependent on a knowledge of
the distance of the target than free-stylers, for with practice
they gradually develop a 'feel' for how far away the target is
without thinking of it in terms of yards. This method is also
called 'instinctive', which is not strictly true for it is a skill
that is acquired, but it adequately describes the way the archer
judges the extent of this gap. It sounds like a very rough and
ready way of aiming, but archers who shoot with this method
all the time can get very accurate with it.

The Americans are the most numerous and the most skilful
Field Archers in the world, and they have recently exported
to us a new method of aiming when shooting bare-bow, known
as 'string-walking'. This is not as yet used by many Field
Archers, but many of the better ones in this country are shoot-

ing this way. In gap-shooting the nock is in the same position for every shot, and the angle of the arrow is altered by changing the position of the pile in relation to the target. In string-walking the pile is in line with the aiming spot for every shot, and the angle of the arrow is altered by changing instead the position of the nock. The simplest way to do this would be to raise or lower the drawing hand on the face, but this would be very inaccurate because there would be no way of bringing it to the same place every time. At sixty yards the archer will shoot in the normal bare-bow way, one finger above the arrow and two beneath, with the middle finger anchoring in the corner of the mouth. At fifty to fifty-five yards the archer will place all three drawing fingers underneath the arrow so that when the middle finger is at the corner of the mouth the nock of the arrow will be the width of his forefinger higher, and so he can still get the pile of the arrow on the aiming spot.

At forty-five yards the archer will place all three fingers underneath the arrow, then he will put the nail of his thumb on the string in the centre of the forefinger, and while he is marking the place on the string with his thumb he will move all three fingers down until the top edge of his forefinger is in line with his thumb-nail. He has now moved his drawing fingers away from the arrow-nock by half the width of a finger, so when he anchors at the corner of his mouth the nock will be that much higher.

At forty yards he will follow the same procedure, but instead of marking his string with his thumb-nail in the middle of his first finger he will place it between the first and second fingers so that the drawing fingers are one finger-width away from the nock.

This walking of the fingers down the string continues as the distances of the targets get shorter, until at say, ten yards, the drawing hand will be three or four finger-widths below the nock of the arrow. The nock will then be level with the eye and the archer will be looking straight down the arrow into the aiming spot. See PLATE 14.

I would emphasize here that the distances given for each finger-width of adjustment are only examples, and each archer who wants to use this method of aiming would have to spend a considerable time learning what combination to use for each distance. There are thirty different distances used in both the Field and the Hunter Rounds combined, and although some of them are very close, like fifty-eight and fifty-nine yards, that is a great deal to learn by heart. Archers who shoot this way have told me that it has taken them a year to really get it right, but that it has been worth it because of the higher scores they have achieved. Remember, this method allows the archer to get the pile of his arrow right on the aiming spot for every shot, which is much more accurate than trying to guess the right distance underneath the spot as gap-shooters do.

There are two drawbacks to string-walking which should be mentioned. First of all, I feel sure that it must reduce the length of life of the bow, but by how much I do not know. When the archer puts his drawing-fingers several inches below the nocking-point it takes pressure away from the top limb and puts it on the bottom limb, so that on every shot made in this fashion the bottom limb is doing more than its designed share of the work which must lead to limb failure sooner rather than later. My second objection is one which my Field friends will laugh at, and this is that string-walking is aesthetically unsatisfying, in other words, 'it don't look good'. What Samkin Aylward of the White Company would say to see an archer draw back the string with his fingers three inches away from the nock I dread to think. However, I will grant that this method does give very high scores, and in this competitive age that is what counts.

The third and last group into which Field Archers are divided is the Heavy Tackle Division. The rules relating to this group specify that the bows used must be a minimum of forty-five pounds draw weight, the arrows must be made of wood, and the piles of the arrows must be a minimum weight of 125 grains. Archers in this group must shoot bare-bow, and they are really the traditionalists of Field Archery, for the equipment and style are the same as would be used for hunting, which the early days of Field Shooting were based on. Heavy Tackle is very popular in the midlands in England, less so in the south. My old friend Cliff Evans is a confirmed Heavy Tackle man, and he believes that anyone who uses less than fifty pounds isn't really an archer!

It will be very interesting over the next few years to see whether Field Archery can catch up with the popularity of Target. The GNAS has at present approximately 10,500 archers of which only a small proportion participate in Field. The EFAA has just passed the 1,000 mark so they are a long way behind, although this organization was formed very recently. Field Archery has more immediate appeal to anyone who is interested in the bow because of the Robin Hood legend, and the bare-bow style is much easier to pick up than the Target under-the-chin anchor. When a non-archer is given a bow to try for the first time and not given any advice on how to draw, he will automatically come to something like a Field anchor. It doesn't take long to give a beginner the rudiments of a Field style, and he can then go round a course in the same group as a top shot, whereas in Target Archery a beginner will need many months of practice at short ranges before he can even hit the target at 80 or 100 yards, and so join the experts. A good number of beginners who have been discouraged by their lack of progress in Target later drift over to Field and pick up the style quickly, but it is very rare for the opposite of this to happen.

One of the quickest people to pick up the Field style was David Hemmings, the film actor, who had to learn to shoot for his part in a film called 'The Eye of the Devil'. This was the last film he made before he became a star in 'Blowup'. We both lived in Croydon, Surrey, at the time, and I was asked to give him some instruction to make him look like an archer. Within the space of a couple of hours not only did he look like an archer, but he shot like one too, for he had a natural eye for distance and had the makings of a fine Field style. If you should ever meet him in a pub, watch out, for he also plays a mean game of darts.

I do feel that if Target clubs want to increase the numbers of their members they must give more attention to the beginners than they do at present. Nobody wants to give up their own shooting, but some arrangement should be made beforehand about what to do with people who turn up and say they want to learn to shoot, instead of just giving them a bow and letting them get on with it. Having a permanent instructor in the club is not always the whole answer, for so many coaches are technically excellent at the job but fail to make Target Archery fun, which is what it should be for a beginner; he can get serious about it when he begins to get good scores. I have heard an evening class instructor say that it was quite usual for over half of his class to have dropped out by the end of the year, implying that they weren't keen enough, but the truth is that he was not able to keep their interest. This annoys me so much, for archers who are lost in this way will never return to the sport, yet with a better introduction they could have had a lifetime of enjoyment from shooting with the bow.

The limiting factor to Field Archery will probably be the availability of suitable ground. Because of the difficulty of carrying heavy straw bales to the target positions and the hard work involved in clearing shooting lanes through woods, any successful Field club must have a permanent course, and this means that only woodland that is fenced off from the public is of any use. A field course set up in an urban area with access to the public will very soon have the bales destroyed by vandals and all the shooting pegs pulled up. It is sad, but it is true. Although Target Archers can have trouble finding ground, any sports field will do, and all the equipment can be locked away afterwards out of harm's way.

16. *Other forms of archery*

If you ever saw the wonderful film version of Shakespeare's *Henry V* you will remember the exciting scene towards the finish where the English archers shoot a vast cloud of arrows into the air at the beginning of the Battle of Agincourt. This type of shooting differed from ordinary archery in that the bowmen were not aiming at a particular target, they were just shooting in mass at the furthest distance their bows would carry, and they hoped that their arrow would find its own target. The idea of cresting an arrow is supposed to date from this period, when after a battle the archers would walk among the dead and wounded looking for their own arrows. When they found one in a body they were allowed to take all the valuables; a rather gruesome form of prize-giving.

Because the archers were shooting at the enemy as soon as they were within range their shafts would be raised to an angle of about forty-five degrees before being loosed, and the arrows would climb into the sky before dropping down with lethal acceleration.

The title of this chapter might lead you to think that competitions between clubs are still shot in this manner, with one club at one end of a field and their opponents at the other, but I hasten to add that this is not the case. It is simply that a similar form of archery is carried on today under the name of Clout Shooting, but it is still basically the same as was done all those years ago, except that now a definite target is aimed at. This is no longer Frenchmen, who are not bad chaps really, nor even an upright straw boss, but consists of concentric circles marked on the ground, the largest being twenty-four foot in diameter, the next eighteen foot, then twelve, then six, and finally the innermost, three foot. As these rings are on the ground it would not be possible to see them from the shooting-line, so a small flag or white disc is placed in the centre and the archers aim at this. The centre ring scores five points, the next four, then three, two and one. It is rather a difficult job to mark these rings on the ground accurately so most clubs tie a cord to the central disc and this is marked at the different radii of the circles. When everyone has shot they all walk towards the target, taking great care not to step on any arrows, and the cord is pulled round in a circle and the arrows are collected according to which mark on the string they reach. As the arrows will be lying nearly flat and will be half buried, the point where they enter the ground is taken for their score. I find this much more exciting than having a target marked out on the ground, for until the cord has been moved round to your arrows you can't be absolutely sure which ring they are in. If you are a beginner you will be well used to seeing your own arrows in the ground, but it will be great fun for you to see that at a clout shoot, *everybody's* arrows are in the ground!

The distance at which the archers shoot at clout varies according to the size of the ground available, but the most usual distance for men is 180 yards, and for ladies, 140 yards, so you can see that it is quite a long way. Because of the age of their sport, archers are push-overs for old-fashioned terms, so they would often refer to clout distances as nine-score yards and seven-score yards. This may sound silly, but I like it, so there! Because of the great distance the ordinary bowsight is of no use, for the bow is held so high that all that can be seen behind the upper limb is clouds. You can if you wish aim at a particular cloud that is above and in line with the Clout, but you will soon find that clouds have the annoying habit of moving along and out of line with your target, so they are not much use. Archers normally put a simple form of bowsight such as a pin or a triangle of adhesive tape on the bottom limb and use this to aim at the flag or disc. As the bow is at approximately 35 to 45 degrees to the horizontal the drawing elbow must drop towards the ground by about the same amount to have the strength to hold the bow at full draw, so obviously, the anchor goes all to pot!

The ordinary target anchor is used as far as possible and the

archer bends backwards from the waist to get the right eleva-
tion, but because he is trying to aim at something on the
ground his head has to be tipped forward in order to see it
and it is this which tends to spoil the anchor.

To further complicate matters, shooting is often 'two-way',
which means that there is a target and a shooting line at each
end, so that having taken their score and collected their arrows
the archers can shoot straight away without the long walk back
to the original line. This makes it more interesting and much
more difficult because the wind will not be in the same direction, nor will the sunlight. Where shooting is 'two-way' it will
be necessary to have two pins on the bottom limb, one for
each direction. You will normally have six sighters, and you
will be able to get on target quicker if you shoot your first
three using one pin and then the second three from the other
pin, which should be about two inches lower. When you reach
the Clout your arrows will be in two groups of three, and you
can decide which pin is best for that direction. Now you are
going to shoot back again, and if the wind is against you your
second pin will be above the first. The original placing of the
pins is dependant on the power of your bow and the strength
of the wind, but the small alterations of Target Shooting are
out of place here, for you will need to alter your sights by at
least an inch to get much difference at the Clout. Part of the
fascination in Clout Shooting is in watching your arrow fall
out of the sky straight down onto the flag, although when you
go up to score you will probably find that although it was in
line with the Clout it has gone twenty yards too far or too
short!

I once went to a Clout Shoot as a spectator rather than a
participant; I think it was Ariel Bowmen at Motspur Park,
and I was at the target end ready to help with the scoring. The
archers looked like little matchstick men at the far end of
the field and I could just pick out their arrows as fleeting
black streaks against the sky, but the sun was behind me and
as they came down into the target they caught the sun and
looked like dazzling sparks cutting through the air. It was a
beautiful sight, and I have been keen on Clout Shooting ever
since, so do go to one if you can, or better still, persuade your

own club to try one if your ground is long enough.

I see that the one thing that I have not mentioned is the number of arrows shot; this is often left to the organizers of the shoot, but it is normally thirty-six arrows. Almost all of my experience of Clout Shooting was gained at winter shoots of just one club, the Royal Richmond Archery Club, but I am sure that the way they run things is typical of Clout Shoots throughout the country. See PLATE 16.

Now let us turn to a form of shooting which looks a little like Clout Shooting, but which is different in its intention, Flight Shooting. This is very specialized and does not use ordinary equipment. It is concerned not with targets, but with distance, for the whole idea is to shoot an arrow as far as possible. Bows for this branch of shooting are specially made for the job and are short and very strong, for this gives the maximum cast. The present record in Great Britain was set up by Mr A. Webster and is 647 yards, which I am sure you will agree is an incredible distance. In America a distance of over a mile has been recorded, but this was done with a foot bow where the archer lay on his back, supported the bow on his feet, and used both hands to draw the string. It's still a very long way for an arrow.

In normal Flight Shooting where the archer stands erect the style used is entirely different to that of Target; there is no aiming at all, the general direction is good enough, and the arrow is drawn at 45 degrees. The loose is very exaggerated compared to Target, for the bow is thrust forward very hard, and the drawing hand is snatched backwards to get the maximum cast. A sipur can be used, which is a long arrow-rest that projects backwards from the bow towards the string. This enables the archer to use a shorter arrow than the draw-length the bow requires, for he can use a 23 inch arrow at a draw-length of 26 inches, and the arrow is supported by the sipur for three inches inside the bow. The advantage of using this shorter arrow is that it is lighter, and will therefore make more use of the thrust of the bow and go further. There is some danger in using a sipur, for the snatched loose may cause the arrow to fall off the edge of this extended arrow-rest, and it is not unknown for the arrow to then penetrate the archer's palm. Nasty! The stronger the bow the greater the distance the arrow will go, and this is limited only by the ability of the archer to pull it. Although there is considerable skill in Flight Shooting it is really the province of archers who make their own bows, for many of the distance records are set up by people who have produced their own equipment just for this side of the sport. Some of the bows used are monsters in poundage, even though they look a little like children's bows because of their short length. I once asked 'Tiny' Lyne how far his latest home-made flight bow would shoot, and he replied that he didn't know because he had not yet been able to get the string on it. It was Tiny who took part in a flight competition at Oxford and lost all his arrows. Whether they went off course and stuck in a tree or whether they went out of the field altogether nobody knows, all that can be said with certainty is that after they left his bow nobody ever saw them again. For months afterwards he had to put up with jokes about being the first archer to make a moon-shot!

The arrows used for distance are also rather special in that they are thin with small fletchings which are usually made of plastic. The idea is to reduce their resistance to the air as much as possible. In the eighteenth-century the Turks were superb Flight Shots, and they invented 'barrelled' arrows which were thicker at the centre than at the nock and pile, which meant that the arrows were stiff but light. Of course those arrows were made of wood, and today's high-strengths aluminium alloys have made it unnecessary for arrows to be barrelled.

One does not see flight shooting very often because it requires such long and straight fields, but there is always one after the National Target Championships at Oxford. There are classifications for Flight Shooting; for Master Flight Shot a man must reach 440 yards and a lady 340 yards, and for First Class Flight shot a man must reach 375 yards, a lady 275 yards. These distances sound poor compared to the National Record, but my goodness, when you have a go you will find that these distances are not so easy as they sound.

A form of shooting which uses a little bit of Field, Flight, and Clout is Archery Golf, where archers can take part in a straight match against golfers. The archer's target is a white disc four inches in diameter which is placed fairly close to the hole, and the archer has to hit this in less shots than it takes the golfer to sink the ball. A flight arrow is useful for the first shot to get as near to the green as possible. If the green is a very long way off then a Flight style would be a help, but if it is within your bow range then the more accurate Clout shooting should be used. After this first, long-distance shot, it is useful to have some 'putting' arrows, which are old tournament arrows shafts that you no longer need with a hole drilled in the front of the pile to take a three-inch nail or other spike. An ordinary arrow which misses the disc by a couple of inches may skid on for twenty or thirty yards, but an arrow fitted with this spike will stick in the ground and leave you with a short putt to finish.

I am fairly certain that a bare-bow Field Archer would do better at this than a Target Archer or free styler, because shooting 'instinctively' gives the archer a much better judgement of distance which is so important as the archer gets near to the hole.

When the archer shoots into the rough or into a bunker he incurs an extra stroke, because he has no difficulty in taking the next shot from there, whereas the golfer might find it difficult to get out. Ask any golfer! Apart from this the rules are exactly the same as in golf. It can be played just among archers, or it can take place on a proper course against a team of golfers, but whichever you are doing, please take care over the safety side of things. A golf ball can give a very hard blow, but to be struck by an arrow is much worse, so do be extra careful.

During the winter months when the interest of your members could slacken off you may like to introduce Archery Darts to the club. This is played in the same way as ordinary darts, but the archers use a face 30 inches in diameter and shoot at it from a distance of forty to forty-five feet, depending on the size of the hall, for it is an indoor game. My own club, the Crystal Palace Bowmen, frequently shoots against the local social clubs, and we always get a good attendance, for a few drinks and plenty of good-natured banter ensures that everyone has a pleasant evening. Although the face the archers use is larger than a dart board, it is an exact copy, so check on the type of board in use before you play an away match. It is not generally known that dart boards may vary from one region to another, for instance in East London and Essex the numbering is in multiples of five, while in the depths of Kent the numbering is the standard one to twenty, but there is no treble ring. There are other variations, but these two are all you are likely to come across. We alter the rules of darts in only one way to make the match perfectly fair, for when a dart player hits the dividing wire between two zones his dart will fall to the ground, so to allow for this the archers do not score any arrows which strike exactly in the middle of a dividing line. If an arrow striking a line is just a little towards one side then it is scored, but if it is dead centre then it is disqualified. When this happens, announce it quite loudly so that all the opposing team and the spectators realize you are playing fair about this.

I know I keep repeating myself when I get on to the subject of safety precautions, but it is very important, and when arranging an archery darts match in a social club *a great deal of attention must be paid to the safety aspect*, for people just don't realize the penetrating power of an arrow. The part of the hall that the archers use should be roped off or at least a continuous line of chairs and tables must be placed alongside the range to stop people from wandering in front of the target, and please give someone who is not shooting, the job of looking out for such things. Before the match starts my club normally put a plank of wood in front of the target and shoot a few arrows through it; you can then see it begin to dawn on people that these are rather lethal missiles and then we don't have any trouble. You do not need me to tell you that the only thing that should be behind the target is a wall or backstop, not a door.

After all the smoke and noise of a social club let's get outdoors again for a form of archery which is rarely seen in this country but which is popular on the continent, shooting at the Popinjay. This consists of shooting at small objects at the top of a mast, the idea being to knock them off. It is not often seen because it is difficult to construct and erect a tall mast. Several years ago my club ran a Target Archery tournament which was televised, and to keep the interest going whilst the archers were taking their scores we had a popinjay shoot. For a couple of months before the shoot we worked at constructing a mast sixty foot tall, but when it was finished we simply could not get it upright. We attached lots of guy-ropes and had dozens of helpers, but the thing just sagged at the end and refused to rise. Eventually someone had a brainwave, and we made it telescopic, with one baulk of timber rising out of two others by means of a series of pulleys. On the day of the broadcast we raised the first forty foot of the mast without any trouble and prepared to raise the extra twenty foot, when we were stopped by the TV producer, who said forty foot looked fine! After all that work! If ever you decide to organize a Popinjay Shoot, be absolutely certain that everyone in the club is as keen as you are, for you are going to need lots of help. Although the most that we could manage was sixty foot, we were all agreed that it was not really tall enough and that another twenty foot or so would have been much better.

The best Popinjay mast that I know of is the one belonging to Roy Skipper of West Herts Bowmen, which he made a few years ago from a surplus US Army wireless aerial. It is constructed from laminated plywood and is in the form of hexagonal cylinders ten foot long and eight inches in diameter which all bolt together to form a complete mast ninety foot long. A thing like this is pretty heavy so it needs a tractor or Land-Rover to pull it upright, but once it is erect it doesn't need many guy-ropes because the bolts keep it fairly stiff anyway. Right at the top is a wooden framework which can be raised and lowered by pulleys, and this acts as perches for the wooden targets, called 'birds'. These are about the size of a cotton reel and have brightly coloured feathers attached. The highest bird of all is the Cock, scoring five points, below this is a perch of four Hens, scoring three points each, and then below this are three perches of Chicks, ten to a perch making thirty Chicks in all, scoring one point each. All the birds have tapered holes drilled underneath them and these are fitted on to spikes on the perches. They fit fairly tightly so that only a good solid hit from below will dislodge them.

The archers stand about three or four yards away from the base of the mast so that they are shooting almost vertically, and they shoot just one arrow each and then make way for the next man. When everyone has shot, they all go round again, and so on, until the end of the competition, which may be determined either by shooting a certain number of arrows or by time limit. The arrows used are all fitted with rubber or nylon blunts to avoid injury and they are fletched with large hunting feathers to slow them on their way down. The archers would normally use their own ordinary target bows, but when the Popinjay is erected at an outside event and the public encouraged to take part then bows of no more than about thirty pounds would be used, also members of the public shoot three arrows at a time at a charge of 5p instead of the archers' single shot.

Roy Skipper's Popinjay mast has been erected at two Game Fairs, and on each occasion over 1,000 people tried their hand at this novel form of shooting. It is a great pity that the transport and erection of the mast requires so much effort, for I am sure that it is something which really enthralls people.

I understand from Roy that in Belgium Popinjay is more popular than Target Archery, particularly in Flanders. Some of the masts in use have cost over £900 and are counterbalanced so that instead of lowering the perches on pulleys the whole mast swings down for the birds to be replaced. Many of the archers use long-bows instead of the modern composites, and the arrows are made trumpet-shaped so that instead of being fitted with a blunt they finish in a flat disc of wood. The entry fees for a shoot are quite high and so are the prizes, for the man who manages to knock down the Cock bird may receive the equivalent of £10. It is several years since I last shot at Popinjay; perhaps I had better book my next holiday in Bruges and see how I get on.

A form of shooting which needs no preparation at all is the ancient game of Rovers; you just get your bow, a few old arrows, and go. I have a friend called Mike Shroll who is a keen Field-Archer, but who is even more mad about Roving, and he will phone me on a Sunday morning in mid-winter

14. The 'string-walking' method of aiming demonstrated by Graham Turpin

15. Mike Shroll hopes for the best at sixty yards

16. A study in concentration. George Brown, Philip Remnant and John McConnell at a Richmond clout shoot

17. Concentration at a tournament. Part of the Ladies' line at the London Championships

when everything is covered in frost and persuade me to grab my equipment and meet him on some rough country not far away. Rovers is very like Field Archery in that the distances of the targets are unknown, but it differs in that the archers choose for targets anything that presents itself, whether it be a tree stump at sixty yards or a dandelion at five. A group of about four archers would normally take part and shoot three or four arrows each, and the archer who gets an arrow nearest to the target scores one point and also chooses the next target. It is best to use arrows with field-piles, which have a shoulder to reduce penetration, but even so, you are bound to lose some, so don't take along your best tournament arrows. For short range shots it is as well to use arrows with fru-fru fletchings so that they do not bury themselves under grass roots too easily. These fletchings are made from one continuous feather about twelve inches long, which is stripped from the quill and glued in a spiral around the shaft where the normal fletchings would go. This gives so much air-resistance that arrows fletched in this manner will not shoot any further than thirty or forty yards, so they do not have enough speed left to force their way under thick roots.

Rovers is a game that needs a lot of open country, so as a town dweller I rarely get the chance to practise it. In these days of growing populations it can be difficult to find some rough ground completely free of people or livestock, so when choosing your targets always make sure that you can see all the ground between you and your target, and for some way beyond. If one of your party goes on ahead to spot where the arrows fall you stand less chance of losing them, and he can also check that there is nobody having a picnic in the target area. The ground that Mike and I use for Roving is a favourite picnic spot in the summer, but by picking a bitterly cold day we get it all to ourselves, plus of course, my wife, Rose, who also shoots but who is mainly there to keep us well supplied with hot coffee.

Finally, a few words on the subject of hunting with the bow. This is something which can cause great arguments between archers, but no amount of words will make someone who is for it agree with someone who is against it. Although a tremendous amount of bow-hunting is done in America, there is very little of it in Britain, and what there is of that is often illegal. An act of Parliament was passed only a few years ago which makes it illegal to shoot deer with a bow under any circumstances, even if it is on your own land and you are shooting your own deer, but this does not apply to lesser game. If you feel that you want to hunt with the bow I would say simply this: become a really expert Field Archer before you try hunting so that you can place your arrows just where you want them. Any archer who looses an arrow at a living creature without complete confidence in himself is pretty despicable. How will you feel if the animal you have shot manages to crawl away from you so that you can't find it to kill it? I know the arguments about man being a hunter and all that, and I can understand that some people do like to hunt, but from time to time I read in the papers about some poor swan or fox being found half-dead and a RSPCA man having to come along to finish it off, and I know that I would never want to be responsible for that. To be fair to the few archers I know who do hunt, these terrible cases that get into the papers are not the work of proper archers at all, they are committed by youths who have seen some archery tackle in a junk shop and having bought it want something exciting to shoot at. I am sure of this because at one time I sold archery equipment for a living, and on two occasions a RSPCA Inspector came to see me with arrows that had been found in a dying animal to see if I could help to identify the culprit. Both times the arrows used were the cheapest sort of beginners' target arrows, very old, different lengths, and not even from the same set. They were obviously a job lot from a junk shop and would never find a place in a real archer's quiver.

To sum up, if you want to go hunting, join a Field Club and practise until you are really expert, and then think to yourself how you will feel if you wound something instead of killing it. If you still want to try, then I wish you Good Hunting.

17. Fêtes and demonstrations

Archery clubs can always do with more money and more members, and a way of getting both is to attend fêtes. Many local organizations will hold a fête once a year, and most of them would welcome an appearance by the local archery club. At one time I belonged to Nonsuch Bowmen of Epsom who were very keen on them, and I must say that during my membership I think I attended more fêtes than tournaments.

By now you should not need me to tell you that the most important aspect of any demonstration must be the safety of spectators. At any fête there will be large numbers of excited children who may take it into their heads to dash into the shooting area without warning, so the ground must be roped off to keep the spectators well away so that if a child does run inside he will be seen long before he can get close enough to the targets to be in any danger. Of course, the area behind the targets should be completely empty ground.

Nonsuch Bowmen arranged their shooting at fêtes into two parts, and their method was always successful, so I will pass it on to you. They started off with half an hour of demonstration shooting by themselves, and after this they would follow on with about an hour and a half of shooting by the public at a cost of three arrows for 2½p, or some similar figure. After this they would pause for a short tea-break, and then do the whole thing over again. The money paid by the public for shooting would be shared equally between the club funds and the organization running the fête, with all the equipment provided by the club. By starting off with a demonstration they built up a large audience which would be eager to 'have a go' as soon as the demonstration was over.

A successful demonstration needs thinking about well in advance so don't leave it all until the day of the shoot. You will need two targets and stands, lots of discarded beginners' bows and arrows, the specially prepared props for the demonstration shooting, and transport on the day to get them all to the ground.

Shooting should normally take place at twenty yards, and even if your team are all Master Bowmen don't make it any more than thirty. The public are more impressed with five arrows in the Blue and one in the Gold at thirty yards, than six arrows in the Red at one hundred yards. Keep the distance short for only Golds mean anything to the public. For the same reason, keep the four-foot face on and don't be tempted to substitute the 80 or 60 centimetre faces.

It is a great help if you can obtain the use of a loudspeaker system so that a running commentary can be given, but give the job to the club comedian, for although the demonstration should entertain and educate, I feel sure that entertainment should be the more important of the two.

A good way to start off is to get your best shot to put an arrow through a plank of wood as I suggested in the chapter on Archery Darts. If the wood is about eight inches square by half an inch thick you can knock nails into two corners and use a piece of string to hang it on the target in the same way you would hang a picture. If your archer can hit this near enough in the middle it will split into two halves which will spring apart with a very dramatic effect. Even if it doesn't break apart the arrow should go through for some distance, and this can be held up for the crowd to see the penetrating power.

While your best shot is doing this the rest of the archers can be dividing into two teams. Ordinary Target Archery is the most boring sport in the world to watch, except perhaps for fishing, so two teams competing, one on each target, will make it much more interesting. Just two ends should suffice, with the commentator talking about scoring, types of equipment, the style used in shooting, and so on. These two ends of shooting in the normal way will allow the archers to get their sights accurately adjusted for the greater precision needed later on.

After this you can place a large bunch of balloons, blown up well in advance of course, in the centre of each target and the commentator can explain that it is a race to see which team can pop them all first. All the archers shoot at once when the whistle goes, and there is usually only one balloon left on each target within a matter of seconds, but it is amazing how long this last one can take because the archers are in such a rush that they often miss in their panic!

You might next like to try Splitting the Wand. For demonstrations this should be a lathe of wood no thicker than one eighth of an inch by two inches wide, and it should be supported on the ground by a wooden cross with a slot in it. This will make it possible to stand the wand about one foot in front of the target instead of fixing it to the face, for then the arrows will chop it down, which is more dramatic than simply pinning it to the target.

Now you can try balloons again, but instead of a big bunch in the Gold spread them out over the whole face individually, but keep them away from the edge which will help your archers to avoid losing arrows. Instead of shooting altogether the two teams use one archer at a time, and the commentator asks the crowd to nominate the colour of the balloon they want the archers to burst. This is very good practice for the archers, for they have to concentrate very hard when they feel the eyes of the crowd on them. Each archer is allowed only one shot, and whether he shoots his balloon or not a teammate takes his place.

Hitting swinging pendulums certainly looks very difficult, and is ideal for a demonstration, but it is fairly simple provided that you can practise it at the club well in advance to get the timing right. The circle part of the pendulums can be made of cardboard for ease of replacement, but the arms need to be made of wood and fairly long and substantial so that they keep swinging for some time after you start them off. They should be pivoted at the top of the targets but at least two foot forward of the faces so that arrows which miss the pendulums but stick in the bosses will not foul the pendulums and stop them swinging. Aim for the top of the swing where they slow down and stop for a brief fraction of a second. Practice will soon tell you at what moment in the swing you must loose, but don't forget that the point at which it changes direction will be slightly lower each time, and remember to aim, not at the pendulum, but at the place it will have reached by the time your arrow gets there.

Your next stunt can be shot between the best few archers from each team in the form of a knockout competition, for it is the old game of Noughts and Crosses. You need a piece of stiff white card two foot square and divided into nine squares each eight inches by eight. The dividing lines should be fairly narrow but dense black so that both the archers and the public can see them easily. You also need some squares of white card about three inches by three which you will need to paint circles and squares on and then push a short length of pointed dowelling through each. The contestants shoot one arrow each alternately, trying to hit three squares in a straight line while the other tries to block him. After each shot the arrow should be withdrawn and one of the markers placed in the middle of the square that has been hit so that everyone can see the position. Everybody knows how to play Noughts and Crosses, and in the normal game as played with pencil and paper it is possible to avoid ever being beaten if you choose your moves carefully. With a bow this does not always apply, for you sometimes miss the square you wanted and get another one instead. You may have to vary the size of the squares according to the skill of the participants, but don't make it too easy. You will need someone near the target to put the Noughts and Crosses markers on, and also to give decisions on those arrows which land on the dividing lines, but tell them not to delay things by being too fussy for speed is very important. Put the markers in the centre of the hit square not in the arrow-hole, which may be near the edge and which could cause confusion.

A trick shot which can mystify an audience is to pop six or more balloons with one arrow. The balloons should be pinned to a stiff piece of card in a tight circle, which is then attached to the target. Right in the centre of this group is placed an ordinary domestic electric light bulb which cannot be seen by the public because of the balloons either side, but is visible to the archer facing the target. You need a good archer for this, but if he can hit the bulb, the fragments of glass will pop all the balloons together, which is certainly startling if you keep the secret to yourself. If you decide to use this trick during the demonstration, erect the target on a large sheet of plastic or similar material before you start so that all the glass fragments will be caught and not left hidden in the grass.

A final game which will give a lot of amusement is another balloon race. Again the balloons should be spaced out over the target faces, and the archers from each team take it in turns to shoot, but this time they have to stand on seesaws and balance there before they can shoot. The two seesaws need not be elaborate, a two foot long piece of floorboard balanced on a small firewood log is quite good enough. Extending your bow arm towards the target tends to upset your balance a little, and this gives considerable amusement to the audience. Try it and see.

When you have done your first demonstration shoot you will get lots of ideas of your own for different novelties, but do try to keep them simple so that there is less to go wrong. If you want to keep the public's interest, speed in going from one item to another is very important, so everything must be prepared beforehand. If you are going to use balloons, then blow them all up before the start and keep them handy and safe from being blown away by covering them with garden netting. If you start blowing them up when you get to the balloon race, by the time you are ready the greater part of your audience will have drifted away, so remember, speed is essential. Remind your archers that they are giving a show, so tell them to look pleased when they hit what they are aiming for and look disgusted when they miss; it keeps your audience interested and it certainly delights the children.

When the demonstration is over announce immediately that the audience are welcome to try their hand at shooting, at whatever price you have decided on, and have a table ready with all the arrows on where your customers can queue up with their money. The equipment used should be light-weight, self-wood or glass fibre bows, possibly donated by club members who have gone on to better things. Make sure that the bows have a simple sight fitted and set about four inches above the arrow rest. Perhaps the arrows are also donated by club members, but quite a lot of them will be needed and some clubs go to the trouble of buying the cheapest arrow materials in bulk and make several dozens which are kept especially for these occasions. Always count the arrows before the start of the shooting so that you can check at the end of the day if they have all been collected or if some are still hidden in the grass. There is no harm in sticking to the one length of 28 inches, provided that the bows can take it. This removes the danger of people overdrawing, and it saves all the trouble of sorting the arrows out into various lengths. When all the arrows have been shot the collection of them should be done only by members of the club, for if you let the public help they will certainly break some.

Customers may be 'sold' their arrows at the table, but the bows should be at the shooting-line, and an archer must be in charge of each one. Never leave members of the public to shoot without supervision, the risk of an accident of some sort occurring is far too great.

As your customers are going to shoot only three or six arrows, supply them with simple armguards that can be put on very quickly, otherwise you will waste a lot of time, which is money. With weak bows, it will probably not be necessary to give them tabs, after all they are not going to get very sore with a weak bow and only three or six arrows. Similarly, although some simple advice on the correct anchor may be given, it is a waste of time to insist on a good anchor before allowing them to shoot, although this may be worthwhile if they keep coming back for more, are genuinely interested, and may if encouraged, join the club. Most of your participants simply want to have a go and then forget about it, so any style will do. There are only two things the archer in charge of each bow must do, and these are to show the method of holding the string with three fingers, and he must check that they do not draw the arrow within the bow. Unless your customer is pointing the arrow at a dangerously high angle it is better not to give too much advice on the aiming; a simple instruction to get the pin on the centre will do. If you say something specific like 'Aim a little higher' you will find that a sudden snatched loose will send the arrow hurtling over the top of the target, and they will give you a withering glance that puts the entire blame on you. Give plenty of encouragement, but not too much advice, and make sure that they come to no harm.

Demonstrations can be great fun so long as the person in charge makes sure that all the archers who arrive to help do participate, not only in the shooting, but in the coaching of the public afterwards. It is not fair if the club's best shots monopolize the shooting and get all the cheers from the crowd, and then all the hard work of helping people to shoot is done by the less skilful members. Showing a continual stream of people how to shoot arrows is tiring work and everyone must take a turn at it.

Keep an eye open for those people who keep coming back and are obviously interested in the sport. Have a chat with them and tell them a little about the club, and if they do decide to pay you a visit, remember what I said earlier and make sure that someone looks after them. Nonsuch Bowmen used to get a lot of new members from these demonstration shoots, in fact I well remember that one of these, Audrey Werge, later became Champion of the County of Surrey and a Master Bowman.

18. Indoor Shooting

There is no official season for Target Archery and many people do shoot all the year round, but it must be admitted that as the days get shorter and colder the less keen, or should I say more sensible, archers put their bows away and wait for the spring to return. It is a great pity that some of them do not return to their clubs when the warm days come back again, but this loss of members can be avoided when the committee take positive steps to keep the club active during the winter months by finding somewhere to shoot indoors.

Most churches will have a meeting hall which they would be willing to let out on one night each week, and social clubs often have one 'dead' night each week which they would be willing to let you have. The minimum range you need for shooting is twenty yards, plus two yards behind the targets for the erection of a backstop, and three or four yards behind the shooting line for the archers. The face to be used at twenty yards is the 60 centimetres, but if you are lucky and obtain the use of a hall long enough to enable you to shoot thirty metres you can use the 80 centimetre face. However, I feel that you would be better off using the 60 cm face at either distance except when you are practising for a competition involving 80 cm, for the 60 cm face is less than half the price of the 80 cm and it is possible to get two 60 cm on one four-foot boss, which you cannot do with the 80 cm. This increases the life of the boss enormously, because by turning the boss round by a few degrees before each evening's shooting, the Golds of the two 60 cm faces will be over a different part of the boss, and this will spread the wear and tear. This does not apply if your club members never get any Golds!

You must erect an efficient backstop behind the targets before you start shooting, for no matter how good your archers are someone will miss the straw boss sooner or later or there may be penetrations, and in both cases it will mean that an arrow will hit the wall. If you make holes in the wall behind the targets you will probably be told politely but firmly to leave. A building material called Strammit Board is very good for use as backstops, and this consists of highly compressed straw between two layers of very thick cardboard. Don't confuse this with another type of material which looks roughly the same but has plaster instead of straw inside and which will ruin arrows quite quickly. The one drawback of a Strammit backstop is that it is so large and heavy that it has to be kept permanently in place and you will be lucky if you can get the owners of the hall to give you permission for this. Most clubs with indoor ranges use an alternative method to stop those arrows which miss, hanging sacks behind the targets, and this is quite effective. If several sacks are sewn together end-to-end and then nailed to a pole by one edge they can hang down from the pole which is suspended parallel to the ground and placed about eight foot high. What method you use to keep the pole in place is up to your own ingenuity and will vary according to the internal structure of the hall, but supports screwed into the side walls or pulleys fixed to the ceiling joists is the usual answer. When shooting is over the sacking can be rolled around the pole, leaving you with a long bundle which is a lot easier to store than several large sheets of board. The sacking you use should be of a type that is closely woven to stop the arrows penetrating, and when in use it should hang loosely, for if you fix the bottom edge in any way the arrows will pass straight through, for you are in effect then making a rigid surface of the sacks. The way in which loose sacking stops arrows is by giving with the arrows and so de-accelerating them. It is possible to buy from archery stockists a special close-mesh nylon netting which is ideal for a back-stop, but it is too expensive for many archery clubs. If you are interested, your dealer will be happy to tell you the price and discuss sizes with you, and you can decide for yourself whether or not you can afford it.

When you have solved the question of backstops you might care to give a little time and money to providing additional lighting, for in most halls you will find that you could do with more light at the targets. At the evening school at which I teach I found that although the lighting was ideal for the ball games for which it was intended, it was so diffuse that the archers could not distinguish their arrows from the holes already made in the target, even from so short a distance as twenty yards. To overcome this difficulty I made some spot-lights, one for each boss, at a cost of about 75p each, and they were an immediate success. Each spotlight consists of two pieces of chipboard eight inches square by half an inch thick which are screwed together at one edge to form a right angle. Paint the outside of the right angle black and the inside white. It is possible to obtain quite easily special bulb-holders which stand at forty-five degrees to the surface to which they are screwed, and one of these is attached to the inside of each of the wooden angles. Decide how far apart your bosses are going to be, and then wire your spotlights together so that when they are placed on the ground each one will be in line with the centre of a boss. Allow a little extra wire between each light, for I made mine exactly the right distance and then found that with continual packing and un-packing the stiff wire was considerably bent and this shortened the distance between the lights. Use heavy-duty plastic covered wiring, rather than the thin, twisted type for it may occasionally be stepped on by the archers as they take their scores, and you don't want any of them to suddenly go up in a flash of sparks and a puff of blue smoke. The bulbs themselves are the most expensive item and these will cost you about 50p each. Al-though there will probably be two faces on each boss the throw of light from one spotlight bulb will be enough to cover them both, provided that it is placed centrally. Although I have never tried a light on each face, I think that this would spoil the nice sharp shadows the arrows throw when there is just one light between two faces.

When using the spotlights there should be some lighting above the archers so that they can see to nock and aim, but turn all the other lights out except for the spotlights on the faces. When the arrows strike they cast a long black shadow on the face which will show you exactly where they are. The chipboard in front of the bulb shields the light and stops you from being dazzled, and it also keeps the bulb safe from damage if ever a really bad arrow should drop that low. Shooting with the aid of spotlights also helps you to keep everyone keen, for when you go into a darkened hall with just the targets standing out brightly at one end it really does look most impressive.

This question of keeping everyone keen is just as important indoors as outside, and it is probably more difficult to keep your members enthusiastic during the winter because there are few tournaments to go to, and they have to make the effort of leaving a nice warm home to come to your draughty little hall. So many clubs start indoor shooting with all of their members turning up regularly, and then by the end of the winter just two or three are coming along. When I first started teaching at evening classes the same thing used to happen with my crowd, but over the years various people have had bright ideas which I have been bright enough to steal, and now I am pleased to say I lose very few. The answer lies in making the shooting competitive, and not just for the one or two archers right at the top, but for everyone. For a start, letting all the archers shoot for as long as they like, when they like, whether it is one dozen or five dozen, is a mistake. There should be a set number of arrows for everyone, depending on the length of time you have got the hall and the number attending. At my own class there may be three or four sighting ends while people are arriving, but as soon as everyone is present (or we can't wait any longer) they all shoot exactly five dozen, scoring all the time and under the usual GNAS rules. Three arrows are shot at a time instead of six to avoid arrow damage, and there are two archers to each face shooting alternately. At the end of the evening, while everyone is putting the targets and backstop away and packing the lights, I can do a quick bit of arithmetic so that I can announce the top three or four scores and also mention the person who has beaten his previous best score by most points.

If you have already made a backstop and spotlights, you should not have much difficulty in making a running-scoreboard for indoor shooting. This should have spaces for nearly all the archers and their scores; I say nearly all the archers because you may embarrass and perhaps lose the bottom three or four archers if their positions are shown, but who won't mind being left off the board altogether if they know they have company.

This scoreboard should not show each week's scores, but each archer's *best* score. Even when they go through a bad patch, each archer can see at a glance what he has been able to do in the past, and this will give him something more substantial to try for. During the first few weeks of shooting you will have a lot of work to do in keeping the scoreboard up to date, with the scores all increasing and archers changing their positions; but this will get less with time so that each week there will be only two or three that need altering.

It is worthwhile thinking up some award to be given to each archer as soon as he reaches some high but attainable standard. At my class we shoot five dozen arrows at a 60 cm face from 20 yards, and a score of 500 is thought to be pretty good for the average member, so for this we present a red badge with a black figure 500 painted on it, as well as changing that archer's score on the board from white to red. It is only a little badge costing a few pence to make, but it is amazing how hard an archer will try when his previous best score is 499!

An excellent idea stolen from America is to put archers together with others of the same standard so that they are evenly matched and can fight it out end by end. On the first target we put the best four archers, on the second target the next best four, and so on down the line. This is done on current shooting form rather than the previous best shown on the board, for an archer's ability can vary considerably during the winter months, and he could be badly mismatched to his companions. Simply put the last week's scoresheets in order of merit and read the names out in batches of whatever size you are using. This also helps to get everyone to know each other.

The final thing you need to make your indoor shooting a great success is probably the most important. It is difficult to put a name to, but probably 'good fellowship' just about sums it up. If everyone has a good time and enjoys the company of the other archers they will keep coming back for more. The competitiveness will keep interest alive, but this should be leavened with plenty of wisecracks and jocular comments about each other's shooting. Don't let it get too serious, for let us face it, we are talking about one club at the weekly indoor meeting, not the World Championship.

When the shooting for score has finished you may have some time left which you can use for novelty shoots, similar to those described in the last chapter. Avoid games like Noughts and Crosses which are really meant for two contestants, but invent games or unusual targets which can be shot at by everyone. A popular but difficult stunt is shooting out candles in the dark. Use the very small birthday cake candles and support each one on an upright pole in front of each target. The poles must be well in front of the targets so that when you get a near-miss there is no danger of the fletchings remaining near the flame. Turn all the lights out so that there is just a row of tiny glimmers at the end of the hall. We find it best to attach the candles to the pole by means of a long piece of stiff wire, otherwise people tend to put the light out by hitting the pole.

Twenty yards is too short a distance for balloons, but it is fine for pendulums. Nothing elaborate is needed, empty corn-flake packets set swinging on the end of a piece of string will do, but you will need to suspend them from long dowels stuck into the top of the boss so that they are about two foot away from the surface of the target, otherwise the first arrow will stop the box swinging even if it doesn't hit it. Even better than this is to suspend paper cups in front of the targets hanging from lengths of thread, and with a small block of wood in each to give them enough inertia to keep them going. Just start them off and you will find that every time they are hit they bound about so much that there is no need for anyone to go down to the targets to get them moving again.

A novelty which creates a lot of fun is to shoot at cardboard discs about a foot in diameter and hanging from strong cotton, but with a bright aiming spot on one side of the disc only. Each disc is given a few turns to twist the thread, and then as it slowly turns the archers try to hit their own discs, but only

on the side showing the aiming spot. This needs good judgement on when to come to full draw, and gives a lot of amusement and swearing through clenched teeth when the disc fails
to turn full circle and leaves the archer at full draw and aiming
edge on at a stationary target.

Once you start novelty shoots your members will think of
plenty of ideas for themselves, but try to keep them simple.
We have had all sorts of complicated things involving flashing
lights, and ships that sink into a painted sea when cotton is cut
through, so there is no limit to the things you can dream up
if you have got the time, but these complicated ideas seem to
take far too much time to get them set up properly. One idea
I should warn you about, and that is the one of hanging up old
gramophone records for you to smash. They don't smash, the
arrows pass straight through but leave all their fletchings
behind.

Some archers have difficulty in aiming at short distances,
for with the modern composite bows that are in use today they
find that they have to raise their sight so high for twenty yards
that the cutaway section is not long enough and the sight
disappears behind the bow-limb. There are several ways of
getting around this problem, of which the simplest is to aim
at the bottom of the target so that you can still see your bowsight but the Gold is covered by the upper limb. A much better
solution is to use some arrows which you have specially fletched
with large hunting feathers. The drag which these fletchings
will give to ordinary tournament arrows will be enough to
slow them down a little over twenty yards so that you can
lower your sight and again aim at the Gold. I have seen one
archer who still could not get a mark using hunting fletchings,
and he fitted three shafts with fru-fru fletchings which really
dragged them down, although I think he lost a good deal of
accuracy because of the difficulty in matching such arrows to
each other.

There are two other solutions which I have seen archers
using but which I feel would interfere with the matching of
the arrows to the bow, and in both cases this consisted of increasing the weight of the bowstring. The first way is to make
a special one just for short range shooting which has several

more strands in it, and the second way is to use a normal string but to serve it for the whole of its length instead of just in the centre.

Archers shooting indoors should be particularly concerned with safety precautions, because in such a confined space there is little warning if someone should wander in front of a drawn bow. Any doors leading into the hall should be locked, except for any that are behind the archers. It is not good enough to tell everyone that the hall is in use, or even to hang a notice on the outside of the door; there will always be the odd person who wanders in. A potential source of danger exists if the hall you are using has a removable partition across the centre to divide the hall into two rooms. When this is folded into each side to give you the full length for your shooting you will have an area on each side of the hall which you cannot see, and if you allow archers to use this space for getting their equipment ready their heads are likely to appear right in front of your bowsight without any warning. Do make sure that any newcomers understand the meaning of the word 'Fast!' and give them some help in setting their bowsight before they start shooting.

19. Societies you can join

When you first join an archery club you will automatically become a member of either the Grand National Archery Society or the English Field Archery Association and your club subscription will include the cost of joining the parent body. It is not my intention here to write about these two organizations, for you will get to know about their workings as you go to tournaments and possibly attend committee meetings, and their Rules of Shooting and Constitutions are easily available. If you do want information on the GNAS then write to the secretary, who is Mr J. J. Bray, 20, Broomfield Road, Chelmsford, Essex. Queries about the EFAA should be sent to their secretary, who is Mrs D. L. Wilcox, 'Pierscourt', Jenkins Lane, St Leonards, near Tring, Herts. The EFAA also have a membership secretary, who is Mr G. Baron, 30, Erpingham Road, London, S.W.15.

THE BRITISH LONGBOW SOCIETY

This society is dedicated to keeping alive and in use the old longbow, the father of all the modern bows and the type that won battles right through the Middle Ages and was still in use for sport in Victorian times. Many of the members shoot in tournaments with modern equipment and are part of the mainstream of archery, but at competitions organized by the Longbow Society they return to the old equipment, which must be either Victorian or authentic modern copies. Unfortunately, there is no genuine mediaeval equipment still in use. The bows used are stirrup-shaped in cross-section and are fitted with horn nocks, the distinguishing marks of a longbow. Only wood may be used in their construction, with no glassfibre or plastic, although the wood used may be laminated.

Longbows are quite distinctive in appearance, and when you have seen one you will not confuse it with any other type in the future. The arrows too must be made of wood, but plastic nocks are allowed, simply because it is just about impossible today to obtain horn ones. The fletchings must be feather, not plastic.

Shooting is 'two-way', which means that there are targets at each end of the ground so that the archers can shoot as soon as they have taken their scores, without the long walk back to the first shooting-line. This is a much more difficult form of shooting, for the reasons mentioned in the chapter on Clout Shooting. The scores are very much lower than with modern equipment, although this is not so noticeable at the shorter ranges. I have seen an old friend of mine, Frank Woodward of the Bowmen of Hatch, in Somerset, shoot 100 dozens at an 80 cm face from 30 metres with a longbow, and this has included three tens with three consecutive arrows.

In the main, York Rounds are shot, but the members also take part in Clout. It is quite a small society, with about 60 people attending the shoots, and a total membership of 160. Although I am a member myself, I have never yet been to a meeting because my work always clashes with the dates, but when I look through the names of competitors on the results sheets I realize that they are people I have known in archery for many years and whose company I have always enjoyed. They're a grand bunch of folk.

It must be admitted that since tournament archery became an Olympic sport it is becoming more and more bound by rules and regulations, so this little society is certain to attract those archers who are tiring of the modern competitive atmosphere and simply want to return to the more relaxed and companionable form of archery of ten or fifteen years ago. Although it is nice to come top, I am sure that at the British Longbow Society nobody really bothers who wins, the shooting is the thing.

If you are interested, write to the secretary, Mr T. D. Wright, 6, King Street, Shrewsbury, Shropshire.

THE SOCIETY OF ARCHER-ANTIQUARIES

When you have been an archer for a little while you may begin to wonder how it all started, what bows in other countries are like, how natives make the equipment they use for hunting, and similar questions. When you want to find out about these things you join the Archer-Antiquaries, for this society is open to everyone interested in the history and development of the bow and it does considerable original research.

It all started in 1954 when Bill Tucker, a keen archer who writes a regular column in *The British Archer*, suggested the general idea of a society for people who had an interest in the history of the sport. It was obviously a good idea, for the society was duly formed and now has 360 members in twenty different countries.

Each year a first class Journal is printed and distributed which contains reports on the researches of various members. To give you some idea of how interesting the articles are here are some of the titles from previous issues. 'Tartar Training for Use of the Bow', 'The English Bow in Battle from Hastings to Agincourt', 'Tutankhamen's Composite Bows', and 'Analysis of Bows and Arrows by X-ray'. There are dozens of intriguing titles like this, and they are all well written and illustrated. Bill Kinsman, the secretary, tells me that no member should feel under any obligation to write something for the Journal, but if ever a member should come across some little-known information he would always be interested to hear about it.

The annual subscription is only £1.50, so if you are interested write to W. J. Kinsman, 14, Grove Road, Barnes, London, S.W.13.

THE ASSOCIATION FOR ARCHERY IN SCHOOLS

If you are a schoolteacher who wishes to introduce archery at his school, or a youngster who would like to learn archery instead of the sports already being taught, then this society can be a real help to you. It is an associated organization of the GNAS, and it was set up to help with the problems peculiar to schools archery, which are quite different to those of a club.

The association has a great deal of experience in introducing archery to schools as part of the curriculum. It can also help with the formation of clubs which shoot after school hours, and has published several leaflets to help teachers who know little of archery. In the months of May, June, and July it organizes a Postal League in which the member schools take part, and this is shot at shorter distances such as twenty and thirty yards, which are ideal for youngsters just taking up the sport. This league is also open to non-members of the association.

About seventy schools are in the association at present, but this number is growing, just as the adult sport is growing. Membership costs very little, £1 per annum for a school club, and 50p for interested individuals. In addition to the leaflets already mentioned, a regular newsletter is published with League results, lots of useful information, and shooting tips.

If you want help with archery in *your* school, write to the secretary, Mr S. E. Crisp, 'Rangemoor', Stony Down, Lytchett Maltravers, Poole, Dorset, BH16 6AJ. Isn't that a marvellous address! 'Crispie', as he is known to his friends, is a very helpful chap and I am sure that he will be pleased to let you have full details and answer any queries you may have.

THE NATIONAL FILM LIBRARY

This is not a club which you may join, but it deserves a place in this chapter because it serves a very useful purpose. It is a collection of almost all the films that have been made about archery over the years, and they are all available for hire to clubs. Many of the films are owned by the Library, whilst others belong to the commercial film companies which originally produced them.

Many of the films cost as little as 50p to 70p a reel to hire, plus the postage, and they cover a wide range of aspects of archery. There are some excellent slow-motion shots of archers loosing, and others of arrows in flight, both of which will be of interest to archers who have been shooting for some time. For newcomers or people thinking about taking up the sport there are general films like 'The Sport of Sherwood', which give a good overall impression without being too technical. For £9 it is possible to hire the Walt Disney version of 'Robin Hood', one of the best of its type ever made, starring Richard Todd and Joan Rice. Whether you are running a membership drive, trying to improve your club's shooting standard, or simply arranging a social evening, there is something in this Library that you can use.

The Library issues a list of all the films that are available, plus their size and running time, and of course, the hire charge. In addition to this there is a brief description of the films so that you can choose one which is suitable for the type of audience you have in mind: potential archers, beginners, or the more experienced. If you want further details, write to the Librarian and Treasurer, who is Mr J. B. Bailey, 90, Hansons Bridge Road, Erdington, Birmingham, 24.

THE BRITISH ARCHER POSTAL LEAGUE

Again, this is not really a club, but it enables you to shoot against other archers all over the country, and is well worth your club's participation. First of all, a few words about *The British Archer* itself. This is a magazine devoted to archery in Britain, and it is full of reports on competitions, new ideas on the sport, arguments, comments, advertisements for tackle, and all the things which interest archers. It is a privately-run publication, not the official voice of the GNAS, but it usually has all the sides of any discussions that are currently occupying the attention of archers in this country. Now in the winter, when I have already said that it is difficult to keep your club together, *The British Archer*, or the B.A. for short, runs a Postal League which any club in the GNAS may join. Two Rounds are available, the Outdoor, which consists of three dozen arrows at 30 metres on an 80 cm face; and the Indoor, which is five dozen arrows at 20 yards at the 60 cm face. Each club looks at the shooting potential of its members, decides what their scores in these Rounds are likely to be, and then sends off their teams likely totals to the B.A. From this information all the clubs are divided into Leagues consisting of six clubs, then each club shoots against the other five, one each month from November to March. The results are ex-changed by post, and the winning teams for each Round are published in the B.A.

In the last chapter I mentioned how difficult it is to keep a club together during the winter months, but this League certainly fills the bill, whether you are shooting on your usual field or in a relatively cosy hall. Most of your archers will not want to shoot every week during the winter, but almost all of them will come along for a monthly shoot, especially if you are shooting against another club.

If you want full details of this write to the man who runs it all, Mr L. H. Wilson, 44, Hartley Road, Portsmouth. If you want to read *The British Archer*, contact your nearest archery stockist or write to The Editor, 68, The Dale, Widley, Portsmouth.

Index